Writing on Purpose

Writing on Purpose

AN ESSENTIAL GUIDE TO WRITING A BOOK THAT MATTERS

SARA STIBITZ

Writing On Purpose: An Essential Guide to
Writing a Book That Matters by Sara Stibitz

Published by Eyrie Publishing

sarastibitz.com

Copyright © 2025 by Sara Stibitz

All rights reserved. No portion of this book may be reproduced
in any form without permission from the publisher,
except as permitted by U.S. copyright law.
For permissions contact: sara@sarastibitz.com

Editing, Cover Design, & Interior Layout
by Faith Smith-Place

ISBN: 979-8-9851290-3-8

Library of Congress Control Number: 2025901857

Printed in the United States of America

First Edition

This book is dedicated to every aspiring author who has ever sat down to write, deleted everything, and started again. Your determination to share your story, your knowledge, and your wisdom with the world makes this work meaningful. May these pages help light your path.

This book comes with access to downloadable templates and guides. To get them—and to get writing support—go to sarastibitz.com.

Scan me

Contents

Introduction	1
Part 1 - Foundation Work	**5**
One - Decipher Your Goals and Motives	7
Two - Choose Your Publishing Path	22
Three - Defining Your Audience	35
Four - The Premise and the Promise	50
Part 2 - The Blueprint	**67**
Five - From Experience to Knowledge	69
Six - Choose Your Book's Architecture	84
Seven - Build Your Outline	93
Part 3 - Breaking Ground	**111**
Eight - Create Your Writing Plan	113
Nine - Navigate the Creative Journey	128
Part 4 - Refining the Form	**147**
Ten - Developmental Review	149
Eleven - Line Review	157
Twelve - Editing and Feedback	166
Thirteen - Crossing the Finish Line	178
Conclusion: A Final Word of Advice	**183**
Acknowledgments	185
Endnotes	189
Writing Tools & Resources	191

Introduction

Most first-time authors think of writing their book like climbing a mountain. They stand at the base and look up, thinking about how far they have to go until they reach the summit. The process might seem hard, frustrating, and completely foreign, especially since that summit is way off in the distance and a little hard to see. And while you might feel excited about your book idea and how it will contribute to your future, the road to getting there might seem terrifying.

Book writing is hard work—make no mistake about it. It has the potential to bring out every single insecurity you've ever had, all the fear and anxiety... But it can also bring out all the greatness you have in you. I know this firsthand as an accidental writer who never aspired to this path; I became a writer due to circumstance, exposure, and time. Over the last two decades, I've evolved from working in the legal field to becoming a professional writer and editor, serving as a book doctor for struggling manuscripts, and ghostwriting *New York Times* and *Wall Street Journal* bestsellers. Through it all, I've witnessed how the process of writing transforms authors into better thinkers and creators. I've seen what works and what doesn't across dozens of successful books, and my hope is to share the best of what I've learned to help you navigate this uniquely transformative journey.

This book is meant for those writing nonfiction books with the goal of sharing life experiences (via memoir) or knowledge and wisdom about a specific topic (via how-to, self-help, education, etc.). Many of my clients include entrepreneurs and business owners who want to grow their businesses, CEOs who want to expand their reach, professors who want to add credibility to their ideas, yoga teachers who want to write memoirs, and spiritual teachers who want to pass on timeless wisdom. While readers writing in different genres will certainly get something out of the advice shared here, I want to be clear that some of this advice will not apply to you. Please feel free to take what works for you and leave the rest.

Also, if you're looking for guidance on how to write with AI, this is not that book. While I'm a firm supporter of using AI as a thought partner, the landscape of AI in writing is evolving so rapidly that it defies the permanence of print. Rather than chase a moving target, I've chosen to focus on the timeless principles and proven methods any writer should learn anyway. This book is about the craft, clarity, and courage it takes to write something enduring—tools that will serve you whether you collaborate with AI or write entirely on your own.

My promise is that by the time you finish this book, you'll have what you need to organize, write, and revise your book. However, my hope is to go further than that. After guiding writers through this process, I've seen firsthand that writing a book is just as much about managing the creative emotional rollercoaster as it is about writing. Most book projects fail not because the writer couldn't write, but because they couldn't get through all the emotional roadblocks that naturally arise during this process. For that reason, this book will provide both step-by-step guidance for writing your book and guidance for managing expectations, understanding your emotions, setting healthy writing habits, and dealing with the emotional ups and downs of becoming an author.

While writing a book is a challenging journey, I've learned that there are many moments along the way that give you the opportunity to rest, celebrate, take stock of what's working and what's not, and prepare for the next part of the journey. Those mini moments are easy to miss if you haven't done this before—they're almost hidden. But reaching these milestones makes the difference between a writer who reaches the destination happy and one who arrives completely worn out, unable to enjoy the view. Consider the space between each chapter and the activities within it your invitation to rest and celebrate along the way.

When you take it one milestone at a time instead of looking only for the final goal, you go faster, you experience more ease and less stress, and you ensure you're writing the book you were meant to write (not the one everyone else expects you to write). Not to mention that you might enjoy the process a whole lot more.

Here's how we'll break down this journey:

In Part 1, we'll do the heavy lifting that will set you up for success. Most authors get so excited about writing a book that they don't stop to ask themselves the big questions—the answers to which have an incredible influence on the outcome of the project. We'll talk about motives and goals, publishing paths, audiences, and the premise and promise of your book.

In Part 2, we'll help you create your teaching frameworks and book structures. We'll also design your outline, whether you're starting from scratch or have tons of writing to organize.

In Part 3, we'll talk about how to navigate the creative journey by setting reasonable goals, creating a workable writing plan, and busting through creative blocks.

In Part 4, we'll walk through revising your draft and go over working with editors and beta readers.

The process I'm about to share with you appears very linear—first you do this step, then this step, then this one. This makes the book easy to read and easy for you to digest. But the map is not the territory. Don't let the order of events fool you. These steps don't always occur in this order. Writers revisit their reason for writing the book all the time. They reconsider their audience. They re-order their structure. Maybe they start without any structure and figure it out after they find themselves with enough words to make a book. It's messy, and it's rarely linear. All of it is valid. Some ways are harder than others, and each way presents pros and cons. In the end, what works best is what helps you write the book.

You'll notice this book is rather to the point. I did this on purpose because, let me tell you, reading a book about writing is not writing. Washing dishes while thinking about writing is not writing (that's just efficient procrastination). Talking about writing is not writing. Attending a class on writing is not writing (unless you have ample time for writing in class, which is rare). There is only one thing that is writing: the act of putting your butt in your chair, placing your hands over your keyboard or notebook, and putting your thoughts to paper. For that reason, this book is a quick read, designed to give you enough to get started. In fact, if you feel driven to start three pages in, feel free to put the book down and write.

I hope this book inspires you to write. I hope you use this book until it's dog-eared, marked-up, and well-used. And most of all, I hope it helps you share the depth of your wisdom and ideas with the world.

PART 1
FOUNDATION WORK

Every book begins long before the first words hit the page. It starts as an idea, a flicker of inspiration, a feeling that something needs to be said. But before a book can take shape, before sentences can form and pages can be filled, a writer must grapple with a deeper question: Why am I writing this?

The answer to this question and the questions that follow it—if left unexamined—have the power to guide you forward or hold you back. A book written with clarity of purpose stands a greater chance of reaching the right audience, making an impact, and sustaining your motivation and excitement through the inevitable creative highs and lows. On the other hand, uncertainty about your reasons, your goals, or your audience can quietly sabotage the process, turning the experience into an exercise in frustration.

In this section, we'll explore the foundational questions that will shape your book's success. What is your true motive for writing? What do you hope to achieve? Who is this book really for? These aren't abstract considerations; they are the compass points that will determine whether your book moves forward with direction—or stalls before it ever truly begins.

Before we build a structure, we need to lay the foundation. Let's start by asking the questions that matter most.

chapter 1

Decipher Your Goals and Motives

"This book won't count for anything unless it's a *New York Times* bestseller," my ghostwriting client—let's call her Lindsey—told me one afternoon. We were two months from the launch date, and she was worried. Would it do well? Would it do what she wanted it to do? These were natural questions to ask, but her judgment about whether the book would have any merit without that particular stamp of approval had me worried.

"Is that the benchmark for success? Why?" I asked.

"Because that way those fuckers will know that they messed with the wrong woman," Lindsey said. By "those fuckers," she was referring to the colleagues who had ousted her from her very successful global business, a story we told at length in the book. Lindsey was understandably still angry and hurt about the scenario... and now she wanted revenge. And she thought that revenge would be best served in the form of a bestselling book.

Let's pause and go back to the moment where the idea for this book was first conceived. Lindsey was an incredibly successful entrepreneur. She was hard-charging, smart, scrappy, and funny. She was not a writer and had never even dreamt of writing a book. But one day, a literary agent saw a story about her in Forbes magazine and reached out, telling Lindsey that she should write a book. When Lindsey told her she wasn't a writer, the agent said, "No problem. We'll just hire a ghostwriter."

Fast forward two years, two ghostwriters later (I was the second), one court case with the first ghostwriter, and a brutal ousting from her own company by her investors—all of which took place while she wrote the book—and one can see why she was a bit burned on the project.

Why did this project go awry? She had so much going for her—a great story, the resources to get it written and published, and plenty of name recognition to get her book out there. But it all came down to one thing: she was completely unclear on her motives for writing this book. Then when all hell broke loose in the midst of the project, she decided to use the book to get back at the people who hurt her.

When the book failed to hit the *New York Times* (NYT) bestseller list, she was so disgusted with the situation that she wanted nothing to do with all of the hard work she put into it.

Here was the sneaky thing about her motives. She was only half aware of them and how they were affecting her approach to this project. If you had asked Lindsey if her primary reason for publishing the book was to "get revenge," she would have said, "Of course not!" and told you that she wanted to show women that they could do what she did. But revenge was all she talked about in our day-to-day conversations. And she got the surface level goal that she said she wanted—she gets messages from women all over the world who tell her how much her book inspired them. For better or for worse, that wasn't what she *truly* wanted. Lindsey is actually a wonderful, warm person who didn't know her lesser motives were running the show.

This is an extreme example, I know. You might not traditionally publish. You probably don't have investors ousting you from your own company. The blow-by-blow is not important. This story still applies to you because what matters is the motive. From the very beginning, she lacked clarity about why she was writing this book. Someone told her she should, so she did. When it got hard, she stuck to it because of the amount of money that had already been spent on the endeavor.

That's a reasonable decision but not necessarily the right one. Then when shit really hit the fan, her motive turned to revenge. Oddly, this kept her going, but when she didn't get the outcome she wanted, her world crumbled. In the end, her unclear motives didn't help her. They torpedoed her.

We're going to start by getting clear about why you want to write this book. We're going to talk about *all* of the motives you have around this book, even the ones that would be embarrassing to say out loud.

By bringing it all to the surface before you start, you stand a better chance of using your motives to get you to the finish line, rather than getting clotheslined by your motive.

MOTIVES

Getting clear about your motives is a major differentiator between authors who get the book done and authors who don't. You might be tempted to only admit the motives that are squeaky clean and noble. Avoid that temptation. Be as real as you can be with yourself.

In her incredible book *Negotiating With the Dead: a Writer on Writing*, Margaret Atwood asked professional writers she knew why they wrote. Here, edited for brevity and bulleted for readability, is the list she came up with:

- To record the world as it is
- To set down the past before it is forgotten
- To satisfy my desire for revenge
- Because I knew I had to keep writing or else I would die
- To produce order out of chaos
- To delight and instruct
- To please myself
- To express myself
- To hold a mirror up to the reader
- To defend the human spirit, and human integrity and honor
- To make money so my children could have shoes
- To show the bastards
- Because to create is human
- Because to create is Godlike
- Because I hated the idea of having a job
- To make myself appear more interesting than I actually was
- To experiment with new forms of perception
- For my children
- To make a name that would survive death
- To speak for those who cannot speak for themselves
- To allow for the possibility of hope and redemption
- To give back something of what has been given to me

Notice the range of motives for writing—from the sublime to the banal, from the inspirational to the mean. Some of the most common motives I hear from clients include:

- So-and-so told me I should write a book.
- I want to change the world.
- I've already spent a lot of money on this project, and I need to see some kind of return.

- All of my colleagues have written a book.
- So-and-so wrote a book, and I can do it better than him/her.
- I want to give back some of what has been given to me.
- I'm going to be forgotten if I don't write it.
- I should have a book for my business.
- I can reach more people with a book.
- I told my [family, business colleagues, email list] that I would write a book, and I'll be embarrassed if I don't finish it.
- I really think this could help people.
- I want to feel the joy of creating it.
- I'm ready to share what I've learned.

All motives are okay, but like my client Lindsey, you don't want any of them sneakily running the show.

Take a moment to write down all of your motives. The act of surfacing and admitting them to yourself takes away any plausible deniability. For example, I'm very clear that at least one of my motives in writing this book has to do with the fact that I am a writer who has helped many people publish books without ever having published one of my own (previous to this one). It's that ironic situation where, just like the cobbler's children without shoes, I find myself missing what I provide for others. So, one of my motives is to finally have a book of my own so I don't feel embarrassed when people ask me about it. Is that a noble, change-the-world motive? No (it's also not my only motive). But it is helpful for me to know because when I start to feel rushed and impatient, and when I start to have thoughts like, "Let's just get this thing out already," I know that this motive might be slipping into the driver's seat, which is not where I want it to be.

Look at your list of motives and determine: are my motives enough to sustain me through the length of this project—and for the next three to five years after I publish this book? Are my motives enough to excite me and keep me motivated enough to continue marketing, sharing, and talking about this book long after I've finished writing it? You don't have to fix them or change them. If you determine that you don't like the answer, this is a good place to reconsider whether writing a book is the right project to invest in at the moment.

SETTING ACHIEVABLE GOALS

Now, the next step in this process is to set achievable goals that will—hopefully—help you cope with and rise above your motives. We're going to identify two different kinds of goals:

1. An intrinsic goal just for you. It's typically not measurable—only you will know if you've accomplished it.

2. A measurable, extrinsic goal that motivates and excites you.

We'll talk about each of these in turn.

INTRINSIC GOALS

> "I want to feel as if I've passed my knowledge on."
> "I want to feel the satisfaction of crossing this off my bucket list."
> "I want to know that I've helped just one person."

Intrinsic goals like the ones above have personal meaning to help carry you through the creative journey. Intrinsic goals are related to inner drive. These goals have to do with the pursuit of what is meaningful to you. They touch on your core needs and wants and who you are as a person. They have nothing to do with the expectations of other people or material success. One of my intrinsic goals in writing this book is to feel as though I've passed on some of my hard-won experiences and knowledge from over a decade of professional writing. I also wanted to have the experience of crystallizing what I've learned so far.

I had a client who found his intrinsic goal through trial and error. He had a major illness which brought him close to death. Like most people who have a brush with death, he keenly felt the brevity of life. After he recovered from his illness, he wanted to write so he could share his experiences—books about business, books about family life, books about the particular sickness he experienced and how he healed himself.

Since juggling multiple book projects at a time is difficult, I suggested he pick one and start there. He settled on the business book because it "made more sense." The book would share the tactics he used to grow and scale his business. We agreed he would work on his outline and send it to me for review.

His outline was good—he had sound ideas, they were well-laid-out, and he had done his research. There would be no shortage of stories or case studies to complement his experiences.

But something was missing. While it was solid, it was like a bag of potato chips left out overnight. Something about it was stale. There was no heart in it. As I read through the pages, I couldn't feel any of his passion for this idea.

We met a few days later to go over it, and I told him it was a well-written and comprehensive outline. Then, I asked him why he wanted to write the book.

He gave me a pat answer related to business and time. It made business sense to write a book. Everyone else in his industry had a book. He was feeling pressure from his family members who wanted him to write the business book. Out of all of his possible book projects, he knew the most about this subject.

I asked him again why he wanted to write the book—for himself. He finally paused to think about it for a moment. He admitted that he had no internal drive to write this book. While this book seemed like the best place to start, it wasn't the book that wanted to come out.

As it turned out, he thought this book was important, but it didn't light him up inside. What he truly wanted to write about was his rather unhappy relationship with his mother and how his decision to cut her out of his life had a direct impact on healing his illness. But of course, it's much harder to write a book about your mother.

Was he really going to air his family dynamics for all to see? Would this help anyone but himself? The book about his relationship with his mother has no business back end for him; he didn't want to be a coach or a consultant or anything along those lines, although he was open to those opportunities.

He simply wanted to write it to close this chapter of his life, record what he experienced, and share it with other people who might benefit from his experiences.

In the short time that he had been sharing some of the details of his relationship with his mother, so many other people—particularly entrepreneurs—related to his experiences, and yet there are few books out there addressing the mother wound. He realized he needed to write this book for himself and for other people, as difficult as it may be to publish it.

We hashed out the storyline of the book. As we did so, he told me he had already written parts of it. Much of what he had already done could lay the groundwork for the book. When I checked in with him a week later, he was happy to say the book was pouring out of him—it felt almost effortless.

So, ask yourself this: why do you want to write this book? This isn't a reason you need to share with anyone else; it only needs to be a reason that can satisfy you, regardless of what anyone else thinks or feels about it. This is not about hitting sales goals, and it's not about getting your face plastered on CNN or Fox News or the major TV network of your choice.

As you consider this question, look for tell-tale signs of excitement about your book. Your body starts to get excited when you think about the idea. Your skin tingles, your heart burns, and you get flooded with so many ideas that you can't get them down on paper fast enough.

You may have an easy experience with this exercise or find it challenging; it might take some time to get to the real reason you want to write the book for yourself, and that's okay. Taking the time to identify your real "why" will save you from writing the wrong book or pushing yourself to write a book before you're ready. Whatever the scenario, write your reason out, and post it somewhere you can see. Use it as your guiding light when you get stuck and want to throw in the towel.

Ask yourself:

What's in it for me on an emotional level?

How do I want to feel at the end of the process?

What big moments will help me feel successful and cause me to celebrate (i.e. when I get my rough draft done, or when I hold my book in my hands for the first time)?

EXTRINSIC GOALS

An external goal is outside of yourself, quantifiable, and achievable. When your goal is vague and unachievable, you're setting yourself up for disaster and disappointment. Your likelihood of success is low, which is demoralizing, and the goal won't keep you inspired and invested when the going inevitably gets rough. Highly successful people like you know this, and yet when I ask authors about extrinsic goals, I get answers like, "I want to make a lot of money with my book," or "I want it to be a bestseller." Neither of these goals are particularly clear or enticing.

Let's look at some common external goals that are measurable. Within the first year of publishing your book, you might want to:

- Book [X] speaking gigs, so that I can... [grow my speaking career, reach a wider audience]
- Bring in [X] amount of business leads, so that I can... [give my team a raise, create more financial abundance for my family]
- Bring in [X] opportunities to teach and/or consult on my topic, so that I can... [become a leader in my field, create the kind of impact I want to see in my industry]
- Sell [X] amount of books... [so that I can earn back what I spent to produce it, know that I've touched X number of people]

It's common for an author to say, "I want to make money from my book." They don't realize that book creation will initially put them in the hole—given the costs of editing, designing, printing, and marketing their book—and the sales of their books may not bring in the boatloads of money they expect.

They need to get realistic and far more specific about their extrinsic goal. Generating book sales month after month takes a considerable amount of marketing work. When you have specific goals with numbers and timelines, they have a clear outcome—you either hit them or you don't.

My external goal for this book includes the following: I want it to raise the profile of my business and my writing (and I will measure that in the number of guest podcast interviews, collaborations, and clients gained in the two years following publication).

If you decide that your external goal is to gain more speaking gigs from your book, you could say, "I want to book three speaking gigs within three months of publishing my book." This is measurable and attainable, and the goal also sets you on a clear path to reach your audience.

Some of these are not so easily quantifiable. For example, if you decide you want to be a thought leader in your field, you will have to decide how that can be measured based on your specific area of expertise. Someone in academia will have a far different metric to reach than an entrepreneur. If your goal is to bring in more leads for your business, you'll want to think about the kinds of leads you want and what kind of book would speak to those people—in other words, how will your book meet them where they are, then entice them to go further with you? Then, you'll want to think about what you have available in the form of packages and services or courses and online assets when they're done reading the book and want more. As you can see, external goals might be easy to identify but need some clarification.

Above all: **Don't set a goal that is actually a dream.** Goals are achievable under your own power, and dreams require a bit of luck and good fortune. While dreams are important to have, making your dream the goal has often ended in soul-crushing disappointment.

Here's an example of a dream versus a goal. Your dream might be to make the *New York Times* bestseller list. For this to happen, your book needs to be traditionally published, you need to launch a full-scale marketing campaign, including PR, and sell at least 10,000 books in the first week and have sustained sales of at least 5000 in the weeks following—those are the rules at the time of this writing, but they change all the time.

Even if you manage to do this, you still might not get on the list. Why? Because getting named to a list is an editorial decision. This means that you could sell oodles and oodles of books, you could outsell every other author on the list, and you could sing your book's praises on all the shows and podcasts in the world, but if the NYT powers that be don't like you, your book, or your message, they won't put you on the list.

Do you see why that's not a goal? You don't control the outcome. The outcome is largely based on the subjective opinions and decisions of other people. I've had a handful of clients who hit all the numbers and did all the right things but didn't make the list. Then, instead of being proud of the incredible effort required to get the numbers (which truly is an accomplishment in and of itself), they experienced crushing disappointment because they didn't get an accolade that had nothing to do with the effort they made or even reader responses to their book.

I invite you to think hard about what you want. If it's a dream, consider writing it down, but then acknowledge to yourself that this requires a bit of grace and luck, factors that are outside of your control. Then, get real about the parts of the dream that you do control. For example, I have a dream that at least 10 total strangers (meaning people I didn't know at the time my book was published) will email me and tell me how much my book helped them. I can't control this outcome—the only thing I can do is work hard to market the book well and get it in the hands of as many people as possible.

Write down your motives, intrinsic goals, and extrinsic goals. Keep them somewhere where you'll look at them frequently—over your desk, on your vision board, as the wallpaper on your phone—so that you're reminded why you're taking on this creative endeavor. You'll need a boost now and then when you get into the work of creating your book, and your goals will keep you clear and purposeful. You can still make the goal in line with the dream, but I hope you truly do the work to get yourself to a place where you can be proud of what you accomplish, even if it doesn't get you where you hoped it would.

A SIMPLE MEDITATION

When I'm walking my clients through the planning and execution of their book, one of the most important questions I ask them is this: What will it be like to hold your book in your hands for the first time?

I want you to close their eyes and imagine for a moment the actual physical experience—picture it in your mind. Imagine the feel of the book, the smell of the printed pages, the emotional upsurge of pride when you see your name on the front and your wisdom between the covers. How do you see this book getting out into the world? Do you imagine handing it out at events or book readings? Do you see yourself signing copies in your local bookstore? Next, visualize how readers will use it. Do you see them using paperback or digital, or perhaps hard cover? Do they use it as a reference or an object of beauty?

This exercise is both motivating and revealing—it helps you realize what it means to you to (finally) publish this book, and that in itself is enough to keep some authors going when the writing gets tough. It helps you realize there is an end to what seems like an endless project.

The bonus to this little exercise is that it brings clarity to a vital part of the process, especially if you plan to self-publish. Most first-time authors experience a lot of confusion and angst over whether to print their books or go exclusively e-book; whether to go paperback or hardcover; color or black and white; glossy or matte; whether to print just a few or go with that printer who tells you that you need to order a minimum of 1000 printed books. It can be confusing, right up until that moment when you picture what your book will look like.

Here's an example. One client told me that she loves hard cover books, and when she pictured her book, she was very clear that it was going to be hard cover with a jacket. She thought that meant she would have to go with a printer who requires a minimum order of 1000 books, which means she'd be paying at least $4000 or more to print her book. But here's the other realization she had: That doesn't mean she needs to order 1000 hardback books. She realized it's important to her to have a hardcover copy of her book *for herself* and to have a few available to give away to clients or friends and family, but she was fine with producing a paperback book for the general public. That means she's free to find a printer who will print the exact number she wants and to use KDP (Amazon's book creation service) for on-demand paperback printing. She just saved herself thousands of dollars with that visualization.

Another client realized he wasn't particular at all about what it looked like in his hands—he much preferred the idea of having readers order the e-book to avoid using the paper (read: trees) that goes into printing books. For those who needed physical books, he would make it available through KDP.

Take the time to imagine what your book will look like when it's done. It's not just about visualizing the finish line; it's about realizing what you need (and don't need) to fulfill your dream of writing a book and saving vital resources along the way.

HOMEWORK

1. **Identify Your True Motives:** Take a moment to write down why you want to write this book. Include all motives, even those you

may feel hesitant to admit. Be honest with yourself to ensure they are clear and upfront, avoiding any hidden drivers that could mislead you later.

2. **Determine Your Intrinsic Goals:** Think of personal, meaningful goals that will keep you motivated during challenging moments. These are usually feelings-centered goals. Write them down as a touchstone for staying connected to your inner purpose throughout the writing process.

3. **Set Realistic Extrinsic Goals:** Define measurable, external goals that excite you, such as the number of readers you hope to reach or the influence you wish to achieve. Be specific to give yourself clear, quantifiable targets.

4. **Differentiate Between Goals and Dreams:** Identify any dreams and separate them from achievable goals. This will keep you focused on actions within your control, reducing potential frustration.

5. **Visualize Your Book's Completion:** Close your eyes and imagine holding your finished book. Picture the cover, pages, and your name on it. Picture how readers will read and use the book. Picture how you will spread your message around the world. Use this visualization as motivation and a reminder of the journey's end goal.

chapter two

Choose Your Publishing Path

When you're starting out on the book-writing path, the options for publishing can be confusing—should you go the traditional route or self-publish? Which is best?

You might already have friends and colleagues who are authors. Some of those friends have probably self-published their books, others have traditionally published their books, and still others have worked with hybrid publishers. You've probably heard success stories and horror stories from every corner, and you're not sure which way to go when it comes to your own journey to becoming an author. So, which publishing path should you take?

The answer depends entirely on what you need as an author and which method will best serve you and your goals. In fact, the answer is so subjective that I considered omitting this chapter because it's hard to give good advice in this format. However, because this decision has such a huge impact on the way you think about your book, it's important that you start thinking about this now. For example, if you decided that you want to shoot for traditional publishing, you wouldn't actually start with writing a book. You'd start with writing the outline, drafting the proposal, and getting an agent (I won't be talking about proposals or agents here, but you can go to sarastibitz.com to download the guide for preparing a proposal and landing an agent].

Our discussion will focus first on a brief description of the different kinds of publishing available to you today. Please remember that the publishing world is changing rapidly; what is possible today may be different than the options that will be available two or three, or even 10 years from now. Also keep in mind that if you're writing this book to support a business, your business model can impact your publishing options. Then we'll dismantle the myths about traditional publishing, since most new authors default to thinking this is the best and first option for them to consider. Then I'll give you a few questions to ask yourself to help you determine what might be best for you. Since we can't cover publishing paths completely in this book, please go to sarastibitz.com for more information.

PUBLISHING PATHS

The following is a quick overview of the publishing path. By no stretch of the imagination is this exhaustive, but it's important that you have a general idea of the different options available to you.

Traditional

Traditional publishers include the Big Five publishing houses (Penguin Random House, HarperCollins, Hachette, Simon & Schuster, MacMillan, and all of their imprints) and the smaller, well-established presses like Houghton Mifflin Court, Workman, Wiley & Sons, and Graywolf. They take on the financial risk of producing the book (but expect the author to contribute to marketing and selling the book). In exchange, authors sell the copyright to the publisher and receive 20% in royalties only after the advance is earned back.

Assisted and Hybrid Publishers
These are publishers that require authors to pay, in full or in part, for the production and marketing of their book. In exchange for fronting the money to publish the book, authors receive assistance editing, designing, publishing, and distributing their books. Authors typically keep the copyright, however, this depends on the publisher. Royalties and sales are determined by the individual publisher. As of this writing, three very reputable hybrid publishers to consider are Page Two Publishing, Greenleaf Book Group, and Idea Press Publishing.

Independent or Self-Publishing
The author manages the entire publishing process themselves and hires people to provide the editing, design, and distribution services needed. The author maintains complete control over every creative and business-related decision. Authors determine the price and the method of distribution.

Social publishing
Authors write and share their work via a public forum directly to readers. Authors might use their existing social media platforms, blogs, newsletter platforms like Substack, or writing platforms like Medium or Wattpad. Authors get to try out and refine new content on a rolling basis and develop an audience over time.

THE ALLURE OF TRADITIONAL PUBLISHING
Most authors start out assuming they should and will traditionally publish. Everything else seems questionable, maybe even sketchy,

in comparison… until we talk about what traditional publishing actually means for their book and their business.

More than anything else, traditional publishing still has the cachet to which we all aspire. The public view of traditional publishers continues to hold them up as the arbiters of taste, the gatekeepers who exercise good judgment and decide what makes a good book. They're not entirely wrong—gatekeepers do provide a level of quality control, and the sheer number of people involved in each book project *usually* leads to a higher quality book. Publishers typically have the pulse of the cultural zeitgeist and a feel for what sells at that time because they are, above all, in the business of selling products. Because of this, media outlets also tend to take traditionally published books more seriously.

That's where the pros stop.

THE MYTHS OF TRADITIONAL PUBLISHING
The following are the most common myths that surround traditional publishing and the truths that dispel those illusions.

"Traditional publishers offer an advance that will pay for the cost of writing the book." Most of the general public has heard about author advances. But what they've usually heard are the examples of outliers—those advances that paid out hundreds of thousands, or even millions of dollars. What first-time authors don't understand is that six-figure advances account for an extremely small percentage of the total advances paid out every year. You have to have serious star power or a well-established name to get an advance in the six-figure range. Unless you've got a following of hundreds of thousands of fans, maybe even millions, you are not likely to see an advance in the seven figure range. You are not even likely to even see an advance in the six figure range.

As writer Karen Russell explains, "Very few of the thousands of books that are published each year will be profitable—not for their publishers, and not for their authors. Seven out of ten titles do not earn back their advance. Most writers will not receive royalties."[1] Even when you do earn an advance, you need to remember that your agent will take 15% of your advance as payment for their services. Also remember that gone are the days where advances were meant to allow the writer to have a decent style of life while they wrote.

Most advances range between $10,000 and $30,000. What's more, they're not paid out in one lump sum. They're paid out in quarters over the course of about two years. So, if you get an advance of $20,000, you would get a $5000 check upon signing the contract, another on submitting the manuscript, another on the publish date, and the last one about a year after the publish date. Five thousand dollars is not a negligible amount of money, but it's not enough to cover your living expenses, nor is it enough to cover the "cost" of writing the book. Furthermore, the publisher now expects that you will invest your advance right back into marketing your book. When you factor all of that in, an advance of $20,000 isn't as kush as it once seemed.

"Traditional publishers will market the book." This myth is hard to let go. "Who else is going to market it?" you wonder. The answer is: you. You are the chief marketer of your book. Gone are the days when publishers did the lion's share of the work to market and sell your book, but the general public hasn't caught up to this reality. Now, publishers look for people who they think can sell thousands of their own books. They make that determination based on the size of your existing platform. Because of this, a marketing platform is often more important than the message or the ability of the writer. If you don't have thousands (or hundreds of thousands) of followers via social media or email lists, your likelihood of getting a traditional deal plummets. A good friend of mine, marketing genius Clay Hebert, likes to say this about the dynamic: "If you need the publisher, the publisher doesn't want you. If the publisher wants you, you don't need them."

Once you get a deal with a traditional publisher, you will be expected to spend an incredible amount of time and money (remember that advance?) on your marketing team and strategy. Publishers do very little to help market the book and often are not up-to-speed on current marketing trends (and will not admit that out loud). While they offer some auxiliary help, it is ultimately up to you to sell the book.

"If my book is going to be widely available, I have to traditionally publish." Up until recently, this was true. Publishers had the lock on wide distribution. That's no longer the case. There are a variety of distributors you can hire who will take care of the process for you, and you can choose how you'd like your book to be distributed.

"Traditional publishing will offer me the best possible editors to choose from." Publishing, like every other industry, has tightened and cut its staff to the point where editors have to wear dozens of hats within their organization.

In addition to shepherding multiple books at a time through the process, they have to manage the egos and emotions of their authors, develop relationships with new authors, work with in-house designers and typesetters, convince their salespeople that your book is the next big thing, and a myriad number of tasks. They are typically wonderfully devoted to the world of books (because who would take a job that pays below poverty level in New York

City if they didn't love it?), but they are stretched thin. On top of that, newer or lesser known authors will typically get the most inexperienced editors of the house. On more than one occasion, I've seen how a well-meaning but inexperienced (in life and in editing) editor can derail a book.

Finally, even when you find that editor that gets you and your book, there's a very high likelihood that the editor will jump ship and move to another publishing house in the midst of your year-long (or years-long) project, leaving you with someone you would never have selected to work with if you had a choice.

"A traditional publisher will help me bring my creative vision to life." Maybe. But more likely not. When you sign on to work with a traditional publisher, you lose exclusive creative control. Your publisher might decide to veto your opinion when it comes to your cover, and they are not known for their design prowess. Or, they might tell you to cut a large portion of the text because it doesn't fit their vision for the book.

They might ask you to write to an entirely different audience than the one you intended. Sometimes this results in a better product for the reader—they're not always wrong. But if you're going for creative control, this isn't the place to start.

Perhaps even more alarming than losing creative control in the design and production of your book is the sale of copyright. When you work with a traditional publisher, you sell the rights to your writing. That means you no longer have control over how it's used.

Let's say you want to use excerpts to promote your book. Your publisher owns your writing and may say no. Let's say you want to use your book as the basis for your blog posts over the next year or two, a totally natural thing to do. Your publisher owns your writing and may say no. This is usually a very big deal breaker for most authors, especially those who need to use their content in creative ways to market their business.

QUESTIONS TO ASK YOURSELF

Taking all of these factors into consideration, you need to then ask yourself a series of questions.

Do you want to make it on a best-seller list?

First, you need to consider whether you have dreams of making it on a list. Now, this is really a vanity metric for all intents and purposes and is way out of the league of possibility for most authors, but we need to discuss it because so many authors dream of achieving this feat.

If you want to make a list that enables you to say you're a "bestseller," and you can't possibly be talked out of it, you most likely have to traditionally publish (which requires that you have a sizable established audience and platform), and you need to be ready to invest tens of thousands, sometimes hundreds of thousands, of dollars into marketing to get on a list. *USA Today* will allow self-published books onto their lists, but the *New York Times* will not.

When we talk about bestseller lists, most people refer to the major, well-known lists, but in the last five years, becoming an Amazon bestseller has become more sought-after and easier. If you do five minutes of online research, you can easily see that maneuvering a book onto an Amazon bestseller list can be fairly easy.

"Bestseller" means many things to many people. Ask yourself what that metric means to you and, more importantly, what it means to your audience.

There are lots of reasons you might care, but your audience might not pay attention to that metric at all. If this is important to you, get very clear about why. Is this a motive (which we talked about earlier), or should it be a goal (because it actually matters to your audience)?

There are a few audiences for which this metric matters. I had a client who is a professional speaker and demands rates of $30,000 for a keynote. His audience is a wide range of people, but one of his primary audiences is meeting organizers and event planners.

That particular audience does care about a traditionally published book. Why? Because the kinds of planners who have budgets that large are typically those who work for Fortune 500, 100, and 50 companies. And they care about the cachet of the book. Furthermore, they care a lot about lists... so, yes, he needs a traditionally published book if he wants a shot at getting on the *NYT* list.

The vast majority of consumers don't care about this metric, however. They're looking for a book that will solve their problem, help them learn, or entertain them. A lack of a "bestseller" sticker won't stop them from purchasing if they think it will change their life.

Does your audience care how the book is published?
Consider the audience that will read your book. If your audience looks down on self-published books (and you need to consider whether they would even notice that it's self-published), then you may need to go the traditional route.

Let's look at another example. Let's say you're a marketer, and you're known for being somewhat of a trendsetter. Your audience is primarily made up of other marketers. You self-publish your book and come up with a creative way to design, package, and sell your book that wouldn't have been possible had you traditionally published.

Do you think your audience cares that it isn't traditionally published? Quite the opposite—it might even work in your favor because that particular audience likes to buck the system and push the edge. They like the idea of a maverick thumbing their nose at the establishment. I've worked with authors in this very market who truly believe you're selling out if you work with a traditional publisher.

On the other hand, if you're in academia, you can bet your colleagues will notice and care about the publishing route you choose. Academics and researchers truly do need to try traditional publishing and get themselves established before they even consider self-publishing, or they'll risk losing credibility in their field.

Do you feel nervous about answering the question: Who is your publisher?
This speaks to the emotional need for validation. A client I recently worked with was excited to self-publish—she knew that it was the right path for her business, and she had some very creative ways to market her book. But when several people in the space of a week asked, "Who's your publisher?" she realized that she hated not having the name of a publisher to share.

This is the ultimate vanity move, but she knew it was important to her audience that she have *some* kind of answer. So, she chose to work with a hybrid publisher to both cut down on the number of tasks she had to handle and give her the name of a publisher to use when asked who she was working with. No one batted an eye—they didn't know it wasn't a traditional publisher—and they all accepted her answer with excitement.

Do you like to have creative control?
You need to consider how much control you're willing to give up.

Some authors are thrilled at the idea of a team of professionals at a publishing house giving their best opinion to make the book shine. That's the ideal. And sometimes you get that, but remember, you don't get to choose every member of that team of professionals. You get to choose your editor, but they might leave in the course of the project.

On the one hand, you don't have to deal with finding and selecting these people, you don't have to hire someone to handle the layout or design, and you're not fielding the minutia of decisions and logistics.

On the other hand, for those of my clients who are creative, resourceful, and like to do what they want without friction, you might have more success and enjoy the process more by choosing another route. When you self-direct your own book project, you are completely in control of every element, including the cover, the style, the content, the design, the price, the date of release, and how it's released.

This is an incredibly important consideration not just in the writing, editing, and production of the book, but in the marketing. If you want the freedom to market in a way that benefits your business, you need to consider your marketing plan and whether selling the rights to your work interferes with those plans.

What's your timeline?
From proposal to publishing date, the process takes *at least* a year (and that's moving incredibly fast), and up to two or three years on average. When you factor in two to three months for writing the proposal, and then another two to three months for shopping it around and securing a book deal, you're already six months in. Then, you factor in six to twelve months for writing the book and then add on two to six months more for production (getting it

typeset and printed). You're looking at about a year and a half to two years before your book hits the store. If you're cool with that timeline, that's great. But if you're looking to write a book in the short term, you'll need to seriously consider going a different route.

Does the price of the book matter to you?
This is one of those subtle but super important nuances that most first-time authors overlook. One client I worked with was excited to get a deal with a traditional publisher. He worked hard on his book, and when it came time to sell it, he did a great job getting bulk sales in exchange for keynote speeches. This was what he wanted—to grow his speaking business—but he hadn't carefully considered the economic impact of the sale price of the book or the fact that he couldn't control it.

When you work with a traditional publisher, they set the price of the book. They will offer you the opportunity to buy it at wholesale, but you (and your bulk buyers) will still be paying somewhere around $15-20 per book. Contrast that with hybrid or self-publishing, where the base cost per book is between $6 and $10, depending on the design and print quality. That means a lot fewer books sold. That means a big cut in what you might take from the sale of your books. If you want to control the price of your book, look to hybrid or self-publishing.

For the majority of my clients, hybrid or self-publishing is the best way to go. Both options are far more economical, they give authors creative control, and authors can take as much or as little time as they need to write it.

However, if you've dreamed of a traditionally published book all your life, your heart may not be happy unless you give it a try. The good news is that you can always try for traditional publishing, and if you don't get a deal, you can still choose any of the other routes. In the end, only you can decide which path is best for you and your book.

HOMEWORK

1. **Evaluate Different Publishing Options**: Compare the advantages and challenges of traditional, hybrid, self-publishing, and social publishing. Consider factors like financial investment, timeline, control over content, and marketing expectations.

2. **Reflect on Your Publishing Goals**: The goals we worked on in Chapter 1 are relevant to your decision about how to publish your book. Think about what you want to achieve with your book and how much creative control matters to you. Using your goals to guide you toward a publishing path that aligns with your vision will help make the process smoother.

3. **Consider Your Timeline and Your Creative Needs**: If timing is critical for your project, take note of the long lead times associated with traditional publishing. Alternatively, self-publishing or hybrid options may provide faster routes to publication. Also consider how much creative control you're willing to give up in exchange for assistance from a publisher.

4. **Think About Your Audience's Expectations**: Ask yourself whether your audience cares about the prestige of a traditional publisher or values the flexibility and creativity often seen in self-published works.

chapter three

Defining Your Audience

Who is your audience? If you just said "everyone," I have news for you. **"Everyone" is not your target audience.**

Your book is not for everyone. If you're writing to sell, convince, or persuade, you need to understand the audience and what it takes to move them. You need to know their problems, their dreams, their nemeses and insecurities so that you can connect with them as deeply as possible. We're going to start by talking about the different audiences you'll need to consider as you write your book.

If you're writing this book to serve your business or career, you'll first have to consider your primary audience. This includes people like your existing clients and customers, or the clients and customers you're trying to reach with this particular book if different from your usual pool of customers. The good news about understanding your primary customers is that you probably already know them well in most contexts. This can be a blindspot though; because you're creating a new medium with which to reach them, you need to consider how they will encounter your wisdom and knowledge in the form of a book. For example, a podcast host can't assume that all of the members of her primary audience—podcast listeners—will go out and buy the hard copy of her book. In fact, it's likely many members of her audience don't even read in the traditional sense. They will, however, listen to an audiobook. Knowing that will change the way that author approaches creating her book.

You will also have to consider your secondary audiences. Let's say you're a keynote speaker. Your primary audience might be CEOs or stakeholders, or possibly mid-level management. The book needs to be written to help them solve their problems. But your secondary audience is event and meeting planners who book speakers for conferences and training sessions. That means that it needs to meet their requirements for what makes a "good" book or a sellable speaker.

My primary audience is typically entrepreneurs and leaders of organizations. My secondary audience is wider and is typically filled with spiritual seekers and folks who are looking for deeper meaning and love my stories. The audience members who really "get" my writing are entrepreneurs and leaders who are also seekers.

There's one more audience that is vitally important: myself. I write first and foremost for myself. Every time I sit down to write, I'm trying to sort out ideas or experiences by putting them into writing. The idea comes out rough, but in seeing the words and sentences that reflect my thoughts, I can then add nuance, refine, and edit.

By the time I'm done, I may or may not have something that is shareable, or usable in a business context, but the point was to shape my own thinking. And I don't share anything that I don't like.

One of the greatest mistakes we can make in writing is to first misidentify our audiences, and then forget to serve all of them, yourself included.

Your primary audience is not the person you want to impress, or your colleague that you're in silent competition with, or your mom (unless you specifically decide that they are, in fact, your primary audience… which is probably not a great idea). Your secondary audience will not buy your book in droves, but they are nonetheless important enough to warrant thought and attention. And if you don't like what you're writing—if your book and the writing in it doesn't make you happy or proud to some extent—you will have a damn hard time standing behind it and selling it.

As you work through this chapter, think about your three audiences and how you can create a book that will serve each of their needs.

PRIMARY AUDIENCE: YOUR IDEAL READER

You absolutely have an ideal reader: the person you are meant to help.

If you're writing a memoir or writing for catharsis or self-expression, your audience may not be your initial concern, and I get that. But I would wager you have that one person in your life, aside from your mother, who adores everything you write because it touches or inspires them so deeply.

This person is a representation of the people who will eventually buy your book. And if you don't do your best to write the book in a way that meets them where they are, helps them resolve their problems, and opens the door to their transformation, they won't know that your book is for them.

Stephen King writes for his "Ideal Reader," which he describes in his amazing book *On Writing*. King believes this is the one person you want to please above all others. In his case, it's his wife, Tabitha. He writes to his wife as if she is the only person in the world who will read his stories.

You'll need to carefully consider who you want to reach with your writing. You'll want to identify the problems your audience is facing, what solutions they're seeking, what they like and don't like, what they respond to, and what they avoid.

Exercise: Audience Profile
Think about what it would be like to have lunch with your preferred client. Consider:

>What do they wear? What is their style?
>Who are their friends?
>Who do they admire? Who do they want to be like?
>What do they want to do with their lives (or do they have goals at all)?
>What do they want out of life?
>What are their habits, both good and bad?
>How do they think?
>Are they outgoing and loud, the quiet genius, or somewhere in between?
>How do they speak? What words do they use? Do they speak multiple languages?
>Are they late or early?
>What kind of restaurant would they choose?
>What do they do for a living, and what do they do for fun?
>Do they have a family?
>What books and magazines do they read?
>Do they prefer audiobooks, hardcovers, or e-books?
>What values or beliefs guide their conversations?
>What do they fear most?
>What are their greatest problems?
>What keeps them up at night?

Thinking about an overall experience with your client can give you unexpected insight into how you can serve them better. Take a few moments to answer the questions above now. This profile doesn't have to be lengthy. You can think about people you've worked with in the past, people you'd like to work with, or someone you've never met.

If you want to work with these questions, go grab the downloadable worksheet at sarastibitz.com.

Exercise: Problems and Solutions
Once you've finished the audience profile, home in on the last question: "What are their greatest problems? What keeps them up at night?" If you can, think about someone you know who fits the audience profile and embodies the typical problems.

Go deeper with this question. The more detailed answers you have, the more you'll be able to hone your framework or mental model to directly address the audience and their problems and give them the solution they crave.

> What is the origin of their problem?
> How do they experience it?
> How does it feel to them to have this problem? What are their thoughts and feelings when they can't solve it themselves?
> What are the consequences of the persistence of this problem?
> What do they miss out on because of it?
> What would it mean to them to solve this problem?

Having a profile of your ideal reader that is no more than a couple of paragraphs is an easy way to keep them top-of-mind as you write. Take a few moments to answer the questions above right now, and you'll have an easier time writing to your audience in the future.

SECONDARY AUDIENCE

Like the keynote speaker I mentioned earlier, you may have a primary reader (like CEOs and HR managers in the case of my client) and a secondary reader (like meeting planners who book speakers for large conferences).

My client didn't have to sit down and think about it because he already knew his two audiences. His business model depended on getting the attention of both groups. So, consider who you already interact with. Are there secondary audiences that already exist in your business?

If not, think about your answers to the audience profile above. Were they clear? Or did you find yourself having to choose between two different Ideal Readers? If so, sketch out the profile of the secondary reader now, using the same exercise. You might be tempted to skip profiling this audience, but don't—they're just as important as your primary audience.

Then look at the two profiles side by side. Where are they the same? Where do they differ? Do any of their interests conflict? Your primary Ideal Reader will always come first. But keeping the secondary reader in mind throughout your writing helps ensure a wider reach for your book.

A NOTE ON YOUR EVOLVING AUDIENCE

We talk about audience as if it's a set thing, as if we don't need to reconsider our audience from time to time, or challenge them, or make moves that might unsettle them and force them to decide what they think of us and our work. We talk about this in terms of static descriptions because we assume that we will remain the same, when it doesn't take much to realize that's far from the truth. I don't know about you, but where I am now compared to where I was three years ago, or six years ago, is drastically different. And my audience has changed, too—the people I want to work with are constantly evolving.

Writer David Moldawer described a theater company that lived on two different audiences: one subscriber audience, comprised of the boomer generation—mostly older, white men. The other audience was comprised of the random theater goers—usually younger, scrappier, thirsty for the next edge in theater. While the theater company was doing well, the shows were terrible. "Pure CBS," as he described them. They pandered so much to the subscribers who paid the bills that the quality of the theater tanked. And worse yet, because they were so fearful of offending their subscribers, they turned away sharp, brilliant shows that went on to become hits on other stages (think *Avenue Q, Urinetown*). This not only led to low morale among their actors and production staff, but it eventually started to suck the life (and the revenue) from the theater company. They had become so beholden to one audience that they were stuck, afraid to make a move that might anger them. [2]

In this case, this audience was not evolving, yet the theater company needed to evolve to stay relevant and keep the best actors and production staff engaged.

Over the course of your career—and even over the course of writing your book—your audience and your needs might evolve. Don't cling to an idea of who you are or who you serve so much that it stifles your growth. Let them evolve.

DEFINING YOUR STYLE

Defining your audience will help you determine how you want to speak to your audience. Every writer has several different approaches to voice. You probably write one way when emailing someone new or someone a little "higher up" than you. You write another when you're talking to your bestie. You write still another way when you're working on your book or your content. Your voice will take on a different tone depending on who you're talking to, how you feel emotionally, whether you're excited (or not) about the topic, or whether you feel confident about what you're writing. To that end, I can always tell when a writer is unsure. It's obvious—the writing becomes choppy, and you can tell they stopped and started many times in the process of organizing their thoughts. When they feel confident about what they're writing, the words flow smoothly.

Your writing voice is an expression of you, so it needs to sound like you and reflect your enjoyment and ownership of the words written under your name. At the same time, the style in which you write needs to land with your reader in a way they find appealing and relatable, which is why we need to give it some consideration upfront before writing.

While it takes practice to create a personal voice and style, consider the following questions to get you started:

- **Tone**: Do you want your tone to be relaxed, casual, or formal? How does your audience speak? Think about the other writers they tend to read and enjoy. What is their tone and style? Brené Brown, for example, has a soothing, warm voice. On the other hand, one of my favorite bloggers Alex Dobrenko has an irreverent, comedic, sliding-off-the-rails style that makes me laugh but is far from comforting. Also consider what kind of tone you naturally gravitate towards writing. Where are you most comfortable, and how does that intersect with your audience's needs?
- **Vocabulary**: What kind of words do you like to use? Sophisticated, difficult, academic words or simple, easy-to-understand words? Do you use profanity? Are you cheeky? How does this align with your audience and their expectations?

- **Length**: Do you like to be concise and to the point? Do you take a roundabout way of explaining things? Do you write in long paragraphs or short paragraphs?
- **Style**: Do you like to stick to the writing rules, or do you frequently break them? Do you use fragments to make a point? Do you vary the cadence of your words, or do all of your sentences look alike? Do you like to use flowery and descriptive language, or do you prefer no-frills prose?

While it's important to think about and cultivate your voice, this comes with one big caveat: Don't try to write like anyone else because you won't ever write like anyone but yourself. Writing like someone else only robs you of your own voice and ability to express yourself. Finding the sweet spot between your authentic writing style and the style that will best reach your readers takes consistent practice and time, but evaluating these questions will help you get started.

YOUR VOICE MATTERS TO YOUR READER
Empowering your writing voice isn't just about how you write—it's about how you view yourself and the value of your thoughts, beliefs, and experiences. I, too, have struggled (and still struggle) with the fear of being seen. I squirm at the idea of my writing, words, thoughts and beliefs open to people's interpretation, misinterpretation, layering, and unconscious ideas about who I am as a writer, a woman, a mom, a person. It's enough to stop me dead in my tracks.

This is not a unique struggle. One client of mine has decades of experience and an almost overwhelming amount of content and ideas. She has a unique voice and perspective, but every time the narrative of her chapters shifts to "I" or "my," she gets uncomfortable. She thinks the focus can't be on her. It feels somehow selfish or self-centered to express the incredibly valuable experiences she has had over her career. If she continued to hold herself and her stories back, her readers would miss out on knowing how she navigated her successes and helped other people do the same. What's more, her stories and ideas are what make the book interesting. Without them, the book gets dry and factual.

I'm a big proponent of holistic creativity—that is, bringing your whole self to the table and feeling free to share all of you with your audience. This can be a challenge. Our respective cultures prescribe accepted ways of being. "Writer" and "entrepreneur" are labels, inherently neutral ones, and yet we attach all kinds of conscious and unconscious meanings to them. Maybe the world "writer" conjures up the image of a pale waif, hunched over a computer wearing glasses and a slouchy sweater. You expect them to be or act a certain way. The word "entrepreneur" usually brings with it the expectation that you are creative, wildly successful, a disruptor, even somewhat of a visionary. You're expected to have both ideas and energy to go the distance.

But what if you like collecting stamps? Is that cool enough for the "entrepreneur" label? Maybe, but maybe not. (Only if you can make it Insta-worthy, *amirite*?) Writing to fit the labels we wear, or consistently choosing to avoid talking about the subjects we're passionate about because they may deviate from the norm, is incredibly boring, not to mention suffocating to our creativity.

Staying in the box of your particular title so as not to disappoint the reader means they might miss out on learning a valuable lesson from your unique viewpoint. The innate desire to people please is understandable but ultimately results in pandering to the audience—the opposite of giving them what they actually need. When you're studied in multiple areas, you can help your reader learn by making connections between concepts they may never have considered before. That confluence is where creativity, deep learning, and understanding take place.

This is why your consideration of your audience needs to be tempered. Writing to your audience can easily become pandering to your audience. When I write, the goal is to explore something that interests me, or a feeling or experience I'm wrestling with. If I have the slightest inkling that I will share what I write at some point, I am already thinking about how this piece will play out in the real world. And that means that my consideration of the audience is already shaping what I say and how I say it. Unless I'm very conscious of it, the brutal honesty is stripped from my writing from the moment I sit down because I am conscious of what people will think of me.

This is a hard balance to strike, and you will have to work out for yourself how you play it. The audience isn't always right. Their expectations aren't always fair, and they deserve to be shaken up at times.

Should you care what other people think? No and yes. Should you write exactly what you want, no matter how your readers will receive it? Yes and no. Only you know what you want to accomplish with your book, so only you can decide where that balance lies. But, I can assure you: the process is a lot less fun if you're constantly twisting and bending yourself and your writing in uncomfortable or unnatural ways to please your audience.

"But Sara," you might be thinking. "What if what I write is terrible? What if what I have to say doesn't matter?" Our fear around the potential for mediocrity, or (gasp) total irrelevance, is ... valid.

The fear is valid, but that doesn't mean you should succumb to it. It's hard to face the reality that what you write might not matter to anyone but you. That fear is strong enough to stop most of us and keep us from writing. If it doesn't matter, why do it?

There's a real possibility that you will care more about your book than anyone else will. But I think we tend to over-exaggerate the downsides and underestimate the upsides of writing and sharing—which can never be measured and quantified, by the way.

One of my favorite writers, the Portuguese poet and novelist Fernando Pessoa, wrote about this:

> We may know that the work we continue to put off doing will be bad. Worse, however, is the work we never do. A work that's finished is at least finished. It may be poor, but it exists, like the miserable plant in the lone flowerpot of my neighbor... That plant is her happiness, and sometimes it's even mine. What I write, bad as it is, may provide some hurt or sad soul a few moments of distraction from something worse. That's enough for me, or it isn't enough, but it serves some purpose, and so it is with all of life. [3]

Your voice matters. What you have to say matters. Your reader wants and needs what you have to share.

For that reason, I suggest writing honestly about whatever comes to the door. Don't judge the idea, the impulse, the story—let whatever comes fall out onto the page. Shaping and cutting comes later.

You can always decide to leave it out in the revision stage if it doesn't move the book along or exposes you more than you like. Don't censor yourself and your voice. Let yourself truly write and express.

EXERCISE YOUR VOICE

There are a few ways you can practice expressing yourself so you can get used to the idea of being "seen" by your audience.

Practice taking uncomfortable stances.
Practice writing out what you believe that's contrary to what the rest of the world thinks. I started a document titled "All the Things I'm Not Supposed to Say," and I add to it whenever the need arises. I usually end up saying those things, either aloud or in writing, but it's a place for me to go say the uncomfortable thing first, to take the stance that goes against what everyone else thinks, and work it out on the page.

Many of us curb our instinct to speak in favor of "going with the flow." We want to keep things cool and avoid ruffling feathers. Good, strong, interesting writing is never going to come from "going with the flow." Practice taking uncomfortable stances now so when it's time to write your book, you've already had practice sharing a contrary belief.

Practice expressing the emotion, even if your words are not well-formed.
Sometimes there is nothing else to do but say what is really there for us, even if we feel incredibly hesitant to share it.

I recently attended a cacao and sound healing ceremony in Boulder, Colorado. As we sat in integration afterwards, I kept having an impulse to share what had happened for me during the ceremony. My rational mind, however, was trying to keep my mouth clamped shut. "This is too personal. Why am I sharing this? This isn't going to be of value to anyone," I kept thinking. I was also emotional, and I knew the words would be clouded by my feelings and the achy sensation in my throat. Not being one for displaying vulnerability in public, I was afraid I was going to lose it right there and break down crying if I tried to speak.

The facilitator was about to close the session when he said, "I feel that someone else here wants to share. I'm going to wait for them to speak before I close the session." The whole group sat waiting in silence.

By now it was physically uncomfortable not to share the words that wanted to come out of my mouth—they literally felt like they were waiting behind my lips—so I finally let them out and shared what I had to say.

After the ceremony was finished, at least six people out of the fifty there approached me and thanked me for saying what I did. Many more simply looked at me with tears in their eyes. The words didn't even belong to me anymore, and I knew that what I had said was not just for me but for them.

There is a cost to using your voice. It might feel safer and less like a burden to keep everything to yourself, but you lose your power bit by bit as you do this. It takes guts to stand up and say your truth, and it might hurt when someone else doesn't love you for it. However, the benefit to using the power in your voice and experiences is far greater than any payoff you might get from staying quiet. Your authenticity is what makes perfect strangers read your words and realize how much they love your writing.

HOMEWORK

1. **Define Your Ideal Reader**: Create a profile of your primary audience by identifying the person you want to help most with your book. Think about their needs, challenges, and goals, and how your book will specifically address these aspects.

2. **Identify Secondary Audiences**: Consider any additional audiences who may benefit from or influence the book's success. Outline how your book might address their unique needs or interests.

3. **Draft an Audience Profile**: Using questions like "What are their greatest problems?" and "What keeps them up at night?" dive deep into your audience's motivations and frustrations. This profile will guide your writing to ensure it resonates with your readers.

4. **Imagine a Conversation with Your Ideal Reader**: Visualize sitting down with your reader for lunch. Consider their interests, beliefs, and goals. This exercise can reveal new insights into how you can connect with them on a deeper level.

5. **Reassess and Allow Room for Evolution**: Acknowledge that your audience may shift as you grow or your book develops. Revisit your audience profile periodically to make sure it still aligns with your evolving message and goals.

chapter four

The Premise and the Promise

Being clear on the topic of your book is easy—you're simply naming what it's generally about. Getting clear on the premise is another matter. This means that you're getting clear on the point you're making. You are putting forward a unique opinion, an argument, a way of thinking that is somehow differentiated from the opinions of others in your field, and you are hoping that your reader will adopt it. In this chapter, you'll learn how to hone in on your premise and promise so you can write a book that stands out from the crowd.

THE PREMISE

First, let's get clear on what "premise" means. A premise is defined as:

1. **noun**: a statement that is assumed to be true and from which a conclusion can be drawn

2. **verb**: to set forth beforehand, often as an explanation

Your premise comes before all of the other good stuff in your book, both figuratively (as in you need to know it before you write) and literally (you will state your premise somewhere in your introduction).

With your premise, you are putting forth a specific viewpoint, one that is based on your unique experience and stories.

Your premise is the beating heart of your book. It's not just what your book is about—it's the argument, declaration, or unique perspective that drives everything you write. A strong premise not only makes your book compelling but also gives you, the author, a guiding light throughout the writing process. Think of your premise as the "hill you're ready to die on"—the belief or insight that you're willing to stand behind, even if it's controversial or bold. Your premise should be clear, concise, and powerful. To get started, try answering these questions:

- What's the main idea I'm arguing for in this book?
- What do I believe that's different from, or more nuanced than, what's already being said in my field?
- What hill am I ready to die on/fight for, no matter who says I'm wrong about it?
- If I had to summarize my entire book in one sentence, what would I say?

Your first draft of the premise may feel too vague or general. That's okay. Keep refining it until it's clear and specific. It should get you excited when you say it aloud. If it's too broad (e.g., "This book will help people be more confident"), push yourself to go deeper. How will your approach to confidence-building be different from existing books? What do other people get wrong about it? What's the unique spin that only you can bring to this subject? Aim for precision and specificity.

Let's look at an example. Here's a premise from the book *Give and Take* by Adam Grant:

> *Give and Take* explains why it's not just givers and takers who occupy the business world, but matchers, too. Givers succeed far more than matchers or takers and why learning to give in a healthy and effective way is essential for a successful career.

In this premise, you can see that the author believes it is better to be a healthy giver than it is to be a taker, and that being a giver or taker is not a fixed personality trait—it can be learned. His premise is not strongly contradictory but expands and elaborates on a long-held sentiment in the business world that you are either a giver or taker.

Here's another premise for Elizabeth Gilbert's *Big Magic*:

> In *Big Magic*, Gilbert shares how creativity is not some nebulous trait that we either have or don't have but a presence which all of us have access to.

Gilbert combats the long-held belief that you are either creative or not. Her premise puts forth a way of looking at creativity using her unique blend of personal and professional experiences.

Getting clear on your premise involves making a declaration about what you believe—and, implicitly or explicitly, what you don't.

It's the last part that can be scary for authors because they don't want to make a declaration that might offend someone or scare them away from reading their book or hiring them. But this is all part of getting clear on what you're saying and who you're serving.

Think back to the "hill you're ready to die on." What is the strongest belief that you carry in your work that is already showing up in the way you talk about your industry and work with your clients, even if you never explicitly say it?

In the process of writing this book, I had to create and clarify my premise, too. Here's mine:

> Writing a book is an intentional act of creating a lasting impact. Writers can learn to shape their knowledge and experiences into a work that reflects their legacy by understanding their motives, navigating the emotional journey, and following a structural approach.

If you're brave, you can also include more declarative statements that show what you are definitely *not* about. For example, I believe good books take (and deserve) time. I believe good books come as a result of patience and digging deep to pull out the best in you.

The inverse of that statement is that I do not support the idea of books that are written in a weekend (for context, this is a common marketing ploy used in my industry). "I do not support the idea" is actually a weak statement. I *loathe* the idea of writing a book in a weekend.

If I included that strong sentiment in my premise, would that alienate people who are looking for a quickly done book? Yes, and I hope it does. Those who desire a book like that are not my ideal client. Will I possibly offend the people in my industry who are producers of quick books? Yes, and that's okay, too. I'm unlikely to do business with them anyway.

While your premise doesn't have to be confrontational or argumentative, it should make clear what you believe and what you will be saying in your book.

Action Step

Take some time to think about the major premise of your book. Try and winnow it down to one to three sentences. Any more than that and you're getting too long-winded. As the saying goes, if you can't explain it simply, you don't understand it well enough.

It's not going to be perfect the first few times you write it out. Take several approaches to it until you feel you've settled on the premise that fully encapsulates the main message of your book and makes you light up with excitement.

THE PROMISE

Next, we'll talk about the promise you're making to your readers. The promise is based on the premise and takes into consideration the problems your reader wants to solve by reading your book. They picked up your book because they believed you could solve that problem. Your promise clearly speaks to their conscious or unconscious desires and fears and assures them that their needs will be met.

A promise is the transformation your readers can expect by the time they've finished your book. While your premise defines what you're arguing, your promise focuses on what the reader will gain. This is often framed as "By the end of this book, you'll…" or "After reading this book, you'll be able to…" Here's my promise:

> By the end of this book, you will have a clear, step-by-step plan for writing and revising your nonfiction book, with the tools and strategies to overcome creative resistance and maintain momentum through every stage of the process.

This promise is clear, actionable, and measurable. It tells the reader exactly what they'll walk away with—not just knowledge, but the tools to apply it. A strong promise also speaks directly to the reader's desires or pain points, tapping into their reason for picking up the book in the first place.

When crafting your promise, avoid vague language like "you'll feel better" or "you'll learn new things." Instead, specify the tangible skills, outcomes, or abilities your reader will gain. If possible, link it back to their initial pain point (e.g., frustration with not being able to finish their manuscript) and show how the book will resolve that problem.

Let's look at a promise for *Give and Take*:

> By the end of this book, you'll not only know how to be a giver with healthy boundaries, but you'll also have the tools to give in a way that helps you create lasting relationships and networks that serve you and your career.

A promise for *Big Magic* might look like this:

> By the end of this book, you'll know how to tune into your sense of creativity and work with it to feel more fulfilled and self-expressed.

The promised outcome is the key to ensuring that the book meets the reader's needs. The promise ensures your reader will know what to do, how to think about a given topic, or what to believe about a subject by the end of it.

Action Step

Think of the promise you want to extend to your readers. Write it down. Think about what you want them to do, think, or believe. Your promise should reflect the thing you most deeply want them to understand by the end of the book—and it should be deliverable. Like the premise, it might take a few tries to get it right, but keep going until you're clear on how your reader's world will change by the time they finish your book.

CHECK YOUR PREMISE AND PROMISE

As authors, we can get so excited about our idea that we forget to make sure that it connects with the audience we've identified for our book. You might think your premise and your promise are fascinating, but let's check-in for a moment and ensure that your audience wants to learn what you want to teach them.

One of the biggest mistakes authors make is assuming their premise and promise align with what their audience wants—without actually confirming the truth of it.

Think of that scene in the movie *The Break Up* with Jennifer Aniston and Vince Vaughn. She complains about how she wants him to do the dishes, and he says he doesn't want to do the dishes. She then complains that she wants him to *want* to do the dishes. It's a small difference in intention that leads to a big difference in outcome, right?

If you have an existing audience, do your premise and promise line up with what they *want* to learn? Or is it that *you want* your audience to want it?

Let's say a breathwork teacher with thousands of followers wants to write a book about *teaching* the method. Maybe she's tired of teaching and wants to license her method. Her premise and promise would be based on what it takes to teach that method of breathing. If her audience is made up of teachers or prospective teachers, then her book might do very well.

But if her audience is mostly made up of people who are simply breathwork enthusiasts, then this might not be the book that interests her existing audience. Now, she could work to build a new audience filled with teachers and coaches, but she needs to be conscious of the desires of her actual audience if she wants them to buy her book.

To avoid this pitfall, reflect on these key questions:

- Who is the primary audience for this book (we worked on this earlier, so use your audience profile)?
- What specific pain points, problems, or desires do my readers have?
- What questions or doubts are my readers hoping to have answered by reading my book?
- With this premise and promise, am I addressing their most urgent needs, or am I focusing on something I hope they'll want?
- If I were to explain my premise and promise to a member of my target audience, would they get excited? Or would they look confused or uninterested?
- Am I trying to "convince" my audience to care about this topic, or am I responding to a clear demand that already exists?

To get even more clarity, consider surveying your audience, talking to potential readers, or reading online reviews of similar books in your genre (we'll talk more about researching comparable titles in the next section). Pay attention to the kinds of language people use in their reviews (e.g., "I wish this book had more practical steps" or "I loved that this book gave me real-world examples"). Then, use that language as inspiration for how you frame your premise and promise.

I hope that your premise and promise fire you up. You should be able to look at them and feel a spark of inspiration. When you get clear on the premise and promise of your book, you can come back again and again to your commitment, which not only helps keep your writing on solid ground but helps you maintain your enthusiasm for writing the book in the first place.

SCOPING OUT THE FIELD

Once you've finished developing your premise and your promise, it's time to think about researching comparable books. It's more than likely that you have an idea of where your book falls in the market. In the industry, we look at comparable book titles for several important reasons.

1. Understanding Market Placement

Knowing where your book fits within the marketplace is essential. This goes beyond simply identifying the genre and category. It's about understanding where your book fits into the existing landscape of books your target readers are already hearing about, buying, or thinking about buying.

Most editors and publishers want to know how a book will stand out in a crowded market. They want to understand what other books will "sit around it" on store shelves or in Amazon's search results. By doing this research, you gain insight into your potential audience—their preferences, needs, and expectations—and you can identify patterns of what has worked well (and what hasn't) in the past.

When you do this research, you want to know:

- Who are the top sellers?
- What are their core approaches and unique perspectives?
- Why do these books work right now?
- Which books are perennial sellers that readers continue to buy?
- Which books were once popular and have lost traction? Why?

Understanding these elements helps you see the "lay of the land" and provides a basis for crafting a book that can stand out. It also helps you articulate your book's unique value to potential buyers, agents, editors, and publishers.

2. Positioning Your Book in Reader's Minds

Knowing which other books influence your book—or which books would "sit next to it" on a bookstore shelf—helps shape the way people will understand your book's appeal.

In the publishing world, it's not uncommon for an agent or editor to pitch a book using "comparison title shorthand," which helps publishing professionals get a quick grasp of where the book fits in the market and why it will appeal to readers before they've even read a page.

You might hear a publishing professional say something like: "It's like Seth Godin meets Chimamanda Ngozi Adichie." Or, "Godin's book *The Practice: Shipping Creative Work* meets Adichie's *We Should All Be Feminists*."

If you're familiar with these books and their markets, this comparison tells you something about the book's tone, themes, and potential audience. Seth Godin's books are known for being concise, idea-driven, and highly actionable, while Adichie's books explore themes and questions about identity, cultural and political intersections, and feminism.

Together, these books create an interesting juxtaposition of creativity and social impact—how the discipline of showing up and doing the work (*The Practice*) intersects with using one's voice to challenge and reshape cultural narratives (*We Should All Be Feminists*). This crossover could be especially compelling for a book exploring the intersection of personal expression, cultural influence, and making an impact through creative work.

Beyond marketing shorthand, this process helps you clarify your own creative direction. It's a chance to reflect on what sets your book apart from others and how you'll frame that difference. How will your book offer a fresh perspective, bridge two different genres, or introduce a unique blend of tone, structure, or content? How will you make your book stand out from the crowd?

3. Identifying and Filling Gaps in the Market
The goal of this exercise is not just to compile a list of books in your market. The true purpose is to identify areas where your book can fill gaps in existing offerings. Every book, even bestselling books, leaves certain questions unanswered or addresses certain themes only partially. By identifying these gaps, you're able to position your book as a "missing puzzle piece" in the larger market.

Here's how to approach this analysis:

- Look for out-of-date information. If a popular book's core advice relies on now-obsolete technology or outdated methods, that's an opportunity for you to update and improve on it.
- Look for unexplored angles. Bestsellers often focus on broad ideas, but niche audiences may be craving something more specific, personalized, or nuanced. Can you provide that?
- Look for deeper insights. If a book lightly touches on a concept but doesn't go deep, you can claim that territory and explore it more thoroughly.

This "gap-finding" process helps you develop a clearer sense of your book's purpose and differentiator—what makes it not just another option, but an essential one. This clarity can fuel your writing, sharpen your pitch, and make your marketing more compelling.

4. Shaping Your Competitive Advantage
One of the biggest mistakes authors make is assuming they're "competing" with existing books. Instead, aim to be a natural "next choice" for readers who already love certain books. Readers rarely buy just one book on a topic—they're hungry for multiple perspectives.

Do you think I possess only a handful of books on writing? Ha! My business exists in part so I can continue to buy books about writing. Your goal is not to beat top sellers but to create a book that feels like the next obvious choice for readers who already love those books.

For example, if someone buys *Atomic Habits* by James Clear, they may also be interested in *The Power of Habit* by Charles Duhigg because the two books complement each other. Your book could be the third natural "yes" in that sequence. If a reader loves *Big Magic* by Elizabeth Gilbert, they might naturally seek out other books on creativity, but they'll also be looking for books that bring fresh ideas, actionable strategies, or a different tone.

By analyzing comp titles, you're not only learning from the best—you're also crafting a stronger book, one that truly adds something new to the ongoing conversation. This approach helps you refine your marketing language, clarify your unique selling proposition (USP), and identify where you sit in the "reader journey" of someone exploring your book's category.

If you go through the comparable research exercise and find that you need to refine your premise and promise, go ahead and do so. This information will only make it stronger.

Comparable Book Research Checklist
Use the following checklist as a guideline for your research.

Write it all down so you can refer back to it later in your process. If you'd like an editable doc, go to sarastibitz.com.

1. Identify 3-5 books that are similar to yours in genre, tone, and audience.

2. Look for books with strong sales (check bestseller lists or Amazon's "frequently bought together" recommendations).

3. Analyze the top reviews (both 5-star and 1-star) to see what readers loved and what they felt was missing.

4. Note any gaps you could fill that are missing from these books.

5. Determine what makes each comparable book "work" in terms of structure, content, or messaging.

6. Look for recurring reader feedback ("I wish there had been more of X" or "This book is great, but it didn't cover Y").

Guiding Questions for Researching Comparable Titles

1. What are the core ideas or themes of these comparable books?

2. What promises do these books make to their readers? (Look at back-cover copy, introductions, and book descriptions.)

3. What type of reader are these books catering to?

4. Where do these books succeed? (e.g., practical exercises, emotional resonance, actionable advice)

5. Where do these books fall short? (e.g., too dense, lacking practical application, too broad)

6. What's the voice or tone of these books? Is it authoritative, conversational, inspiring, etc.?

7. What is your competitive advantage? (What do you bring to the table that these books don't?)

8. What unmet reader needs can your book fulfill? (This could be a missing niche, a deeper exploration, or a more accessible approach.)

9. How will you "sit on the shelf" with these books? (For example, if someone buys *Atomic Habits* by James Clear, would they also be interested in your book? Why or why not?)

By answering these questions and completing the checklist, you'll have a clear sense of how to differentiate your book, identify its market position, and strengthen both your premise and promise. Plus, you'll be better prepared to explain your book's unique appeal to agents, publishers, and readers.

Crafting your premise, promise, and positioning your book within the market are three of the most crucial steps in writing a successful book. Your premise gives you clarity on what you stand for, your promise ensures your reader's needs are front and center, and your market positioning allows you to understand how your book fits into a larger landscape of existing titles.

Together, these three elements provide direction for you as the writer and confidence for your reader that the journey will be worth it.

As you continue writing, return to these guideposts whenever you feel lost, unsure, or overwhelmed. They will remind you why you started this book in the first place—and who you're writing it for. A well-crafted premise, a clear and compelling promise, and a thoughtful understanding of your book's position in the market aren't just helpful for you as the author; they're also the reason your reader will pick up the book, stay with it, and ultimately recommend it to others.

HOMEWORK

1. **Define Your Premise**: Write a 1-3 sentence declaration that captures the core argument, unique perspective, or central idea of your book. Ask yourself: "What belief am I willing to stand behind, even if it challenges others?" Refine it until it feels clear, powerful, and specific.

2. **Craft Your Promise**: Identify the transformation, outcome, or result your reader will experience by the end of your book. Frame it as: "By the end of this book, you will..." Make sure your promise is both exciting and deliverable.

3. **Check Alignment with Your Audience**: Reflect on your intended readers. Does your premise address their core desires, pain points, or needs? Use feedback from potential readers, surveys, or online reviews of similar books to ensure you're writing a book they're eager to read.

4. **Research Comparable Titles**: Identify 3-5 books that are similar to yours in genre, audience, or theme. Analyze what makes them successful, what gaps they leave unfilled, and where your book

can stand apart. Use this information to refine your premise, promise, and positioning.

5. **Refine and Revisit**: With your premise, promise, and market position clear, take a moment to reflect. Ask yourself: "Does this still light me up? Does it feel bold, exciting, and uniquely mine?" If not, make adjustments until it does. Your passion for the premise and promise will fuel your writing process.

PART 2
THE BLUEPRINT

Before you start writing, you need a clear blueprint—one that will guide you from your initial idea to a finished book that serves your readers. This section walks you through three essential steps: organizing your expertise into a teachable framework, choosing the right structural pattern to present that framework, and creating a practical outline to guide your writing process.

Think of it as building a house: first, you need to create a solid foundation by organizing your knowledge into a clear, teachable model (your Capstone). Then, you'll select the architectural style that best suits your message (your book's structure). Finally, you'll draw up detailed construction plans (your outline) that will guide you through the writing process. Each step builds on the previous one, giving you a complete roadmap for your book. By the end of this section, you'll be clear about what you're writing and how you'll write it.

chapter five

From Experience to Knowledge: Develop Your Capstone Model

> Note to readers: This chapter is best for people who are writing non-fiction books that are intended to help or teach in some way, shape, or form. If this doesn't sound like you, feel free to skip this section. However, I would encourage you to skim through it; this chapter is designed to help you think about how to organize what you have to say.

Every expert has deep knowledge of their field, but transforming that expertise into something others can learn and apply is a different skill entirely. This chapter helps you bridge that gap by developing what I call a Capstone model—a clear framework that makes your knowledge teachable and actionable.

Whether you're sharing decades of experience or fresh insights from recent work, you'll learn how to organize your expertise into a structure that your readers can understand, remember, and most importantly, use.

Figuring out how to organize your experience and knowledge in the middle of writing a book is the wrong time to figure it out. It's painful for everyone, makes the project drag on, and builds unnecessary friction. This is the very reason why most people emerge from the process of writing a book and declare, "Never again!"

No one would willingly enter into this scenario, but it's not always obvious when an author isn't sure what to say or how to teach their topic. My team and I once entered into a ghostwriting project with the idea that the client could draw on their decades (yes, *decades*) worth of content—and previous books. They had decades of experience coaching and training people to live better lives. But by the midpoint of the project, it became clear they were at a loss as to what to say... so what went wrong?

They didn't understand the fundamental difference between having content and having structure and meaning. Oodles of content is worthless if you're not sure what all of it means when taken together, if you're not clear about the deeper message—the intrinsic mental model or framework—that brings the content to life.

They hadn't done the work to consolidate their wisdom in a way their readers could use.

They hadn't taken the time to step back, evaluate their body of work, earned experience, and knowledge, and turn it into a workable mental model that could be taught to someone else and deliver a repeatable outcome.

If global organizations with incredible resources and content can miss this step, anyone can. It's that simple and that hard.

THE CAPSTONE METHOD

In this chapter, we're going to take a holistic look at what you've done in the world and where you're going and turn your earned knowledge into the capstone on which everything else depends. "Capstone" carries multiple meanings. In higher education, capstone refers to someone's greatest achievement; the culmination of their work. We'll take your body of work and make it intriguing, helpful, and—most of all—teachable. We'll dive into the deeper meaning of your work and walk through how to turn it into a mental model that works for you and your clients.

STRUCTURAL PROBLEMS AHEAD

After developing, writing, and editing dozens of books at various stages—from chaos to completion—it is painfully obvious that **structure** is both vitally important and a red herring. A crazy high percentage of authors who are stuck in the process believe it's because the structure of the book "isn't right." They believe that if they could just get clear on the outline, the writing will flow. Often, they're not entirely wrong—but the book structure isn't the problem. The lack of structure around what they're teaching is the problem, which is the greater issue.

When an author continues to tinker with their structure without making any progress, it's often a sign of one of two main problems: a.) the author doesn't feel motivated or intrinsically inspired to write it, or b.) the author is deeply uncertain about the core message *and* the organization of their message. In both of those examples, book structure really is the red herring. These problems supersede structure, meaning you need to address them first. In fact, if an author can't get clear about the first problem, that usually leads to the death of the book project.

Let's talk about the second problem: when an author is unclear on the core message of the book, as well as the organization of it.

This is a common problem for people going from "expert" to "author." They've done the work, and they know their stuff. But this step isn't about knowing your stuff or knowing how to execute—it's about knowing how to *teach* your stuff. Going from "doer" or "coach" to "teacher" doesn't have to be hard. Some writers do make this transition pretty seamlessly. But unless you give some thought to the transition, you're likely to miss it and create problems for yourself.

Let's say you're a consultant who has done the work for decades. You've been hands-on, and you have dozens of experiences to draw from. This is great—but if you've never had to step back, look at the magic that you do for your clients, and explain it in a way that others can replicate, you're going to struggle with creating a structure for the book… or for a speech… or for an article. No matter what you're creating, structure and your teaching method are inextricably linked—especially when creating a nonfiction book. One begets the other. When we're unclear on structure, we're usually unclear on the sum total of our work—what it all means—and how best to teach and write about it.

This problem is so common that it can even affect authors who *have* been teaching a concrete process for years. I once helped an author prepare for publication by doing a deep edit and structural review for the book. As I read, I realized that his seven-step process—the process he had taught for a decade and spoken on at length—was actually missing a step. When I proposed this to the author, we both laughed at how obvious this missing step was. How could it have been missed? The simple fact is that when we write an idea or a process, it changes the way we experience it. Hearing is one thing, but reading reveals the holes, assumptions, and errors in thinking in a way that speaking just doesn't do.

This is also a common problem for people who are newer to their industry and haven't had time to digest what they've learned. If you're relatively new to your field, you might still be prone to regurgitating what you've learned as opposed to coming up with a unique viewpoint that comes from your lived experiences. You may not have had the time to come up with original ideas and test them out in the real world. Same goes for people who have almost too much information at their disposal. Podcasts hosts, for example, have tons of information at their fingertips. But if they've never had to sit down, think about, and organize their information into a body of knowledge that someone else can use, they struggle to organize their overload of information into a book.

By the time most new (and experienced) authors realize this, they're already deeply immersed in the writing project and feel reluctant to "go back" and do the work of getting clear. Yes, it can be frustrating, but if this is where you find yourself now, I promise that pausing and taking the time to think this through will save you so much time and heartache in the writing process. If you sacrifice that time, you might even come to think of writing a book as "easy."

WHY CAPSTONE MODELS ARE IMPORTANT

Capstone models and frameworks, words that I'll use interchangeably, take all of your hard-earned knowledge and wisdom and sculpt them into a tool that someone else can use. You've probably heard the phrase mental model, which is a representation, sometimes visual, of how a thing works in the real world. In Latin, the word for framework is *compago*, which means to "bind together." Building your hard-earned wisdom and knowledge into a Capstone model is to bind together what you've learned over the last few decades of your life and come up with a framework that can be shared with your audience.

Models and frameworks are essential for supporting the structure of an idea. We need mental models to learn effectively. Charlie Munger talks about how we need structure and frameworks to truly understand and recall information: "You can't really know anything if you just remember isolated facts and try and bang 'em back. If the facts don't hang together on a latticework of theory, you don't have them in a usable form... And you've got to array your experience both vicarious and direct on this latticework of models."[4]

This is why your framework is so much bigger than the book. It's the core of how you will teach. A very good framework is a tool that becomes the backbone for your book—and your speeches, written content, podcasts, courses, and consulting offers. It should be deeply related to your overall message, the one you plan to work with for the next five years. If you want your framework to apply in all aspects of your business, you need to get the model right before you ever think about book structure. **Knowledge without a framework is useless.**

THE UNDERPINNINGS OF MENTAL MODELS

There are a few key elements we need to discuss before we get started on building your model or framework. First, we're going to consider two kinds of mental models, which we'll refer to as philosophies and methods.

Philosophies are systems of thought, lenses for looking at the world. When I say "philosophies," I'm also encompassing principles into this idea. Principles and philosophies can be hierarchical or come in no particular order (although that can be deceptive, since you still have to describe them in some kind of order). Philosophies can be prescriptive and/or optional. No matter how you structure them, they have to do with the higher-level thinking that is required for approaching a given problem or scenario. This is typically where we tell the user "how to think" about the problem we're helping them solve.

Methods and processes are a set of sequential steps that build on one another, by which a specific task is completed. Methods usually come with their own set of rules, tests, activities, and outcomes which are repeatable. They usually involve action steps to solve a specific problem. Methods are tactical, practical, and far more boots-on-the-ground than philosophies. This is where you tell the user "what to do."

The final result of your mental model should take into account not only your body of knowledge but how it will work for the user. Consider this: If you want to create a set of philosophies or principles, the model will be less tactical and more philosophical—meaning it might be harder for the user to apply in the real world. If you create a process or method, the model will be tactical but might age more quickly as the steps in the model change over time. Process-oriented models are more applicable but less geared toward high-level thinking.

The trade-off here boils down to this: Do you want to tell them how to think about a topic or what to do about it?

Here's the secret: The best models have elements of both. Find a way to incorporate both into your Capstone framework, and you'll be giving your client something valuable.

WHAT MAKES A GOOD MODEL

I'm about to go meta and share the principles of a good set of principles. As you think about how you'll share your Capstone model, I want you to think about how each of these might apply.

Memorable. Books and ideas get shared when the content is memorable. What makes it memorable? Usually, simplicity and portability is best. For this reason, forty-eight steps in a framework is too much. Any more than ten steps, rules, or philosophies is generally overwhelming to the mind, so consider how your steps or principles might nest inside one another if you think you have more than ten.

Outcome-driven/Useful. An empty framework is meaningless—that should go without saying, yet I see rather meaningless models used in sales all the time. Models can be really cool and eye-catching, but if they're not clear on the necessary action steps or end result, it won't create change or transformation. The people coming to you for advice want a specific outcome by the end of the book, podcast, or whatever you're creating, and the easier the change, the better. For that reason, your framework and your book need to be outcome-driven. You need to be clear on the transformation the reader will have if they use your framework—and so do they.

Tested. The framework you teach needs to be attainable, and that means you need to have seen the framework in action. An untested model is just theory. Only when it brushes up against the realities and constraints of real life—such as real people and their habits, circumstances, and abilities—will you truly know if the model works.

Your model should be effective for about 80% of the people who try to use it. Why 80%? First, it's unrealistic to think that 100% of the people who read your book or use your framework will apply it successfully. There will be failures for a myriad of reasons, and that's okay. But there's a big difference between a framework that works when you're standing in front of the room teaching it—coaching stragglers along with your expertise—and a framework that 80% of people can understand and apply with some success without any personal coaching at all. We get to this by consistently testing and refining the framework out in the real world.

This also speaks to the experimental idea of a working model. The model is never really finished. It will never be perfect. It can always be improved on, especially over years of learning how people interact with it.

HOW TO BUILD YOUR CAPSTONE MODEL

When I work with clients, this process is a deep-dive into what they do, who they work with, how they work with them, and the order of steps they take. It's difficult to describe this process because there is no set way to do it, and each time I walk someone through it, our work is influenced heavily by what the client needs, as well as what they bring to the table. Some of them come with partial models in hand. All of them come with boatloads of information and personal experience. What they bring changes the process.

As difficult as it is to nail down, there are some key activities in each process. Remember that this is a high-level overview of an in-depth process that takes time.

When I work with clients, this typically unfolds over several weeks, sometimes months, because they need the time to think about each of these prompts and come back with clear answers. If you find yourself going out of order, don't worry about it. Use this in the way that works best for you.

Step 1: Envision Your Future

Where you are right now is not where you want to be in five years. It can be hard to envision what the next five years looks like, but I want you to try and verbalize some kind of a vision for your future. What kind of work are you doing? How do you spend your day? How does it feel?

Sometimes it helps to first get clear on what you are *not* doing in the future. Think about the things in your business that you would like to move away from and those activities you would like to do more of. But don't stay here—the point is not to create some kind of pendulum-swinging opposite of what you have now but to create something new for yourself.

Some people have a very clear idea of what they want in the next five years. For those of us who struggle with this, you might only be able to articulate some kind of feeling. Maybe you have a vision or a picture in your mind but aren't sure how to get there. Go with that. Whatever it is, get clear on what you're going for—you don't want to create a model that lands you in the same place you are now.

Step 2: Unearth Your Beliefs

What strong beliefs do you have that you are willing to stand by, argue for, and go head-to-head with your colleagues or clients over because you hold them so dear?

Rarely do people take the time to articulate the beliefs that define and subconsciously influence their work. Beliefs dictate your daily decisions, whether you're aware of them or not. Beliefs about our profession and our industry take time and experience to develop, but once they do, they start directing our decisions in business. The first step in this experience is to take time to unearth and explore the beliefs that have developed over a lifetime of experience in your field.

What is the hill you're ready to die on? What strong beliefs do you have that you are willing to stand by, argue for, and go head-to-head with your colleagues or clients over because you hold them so dear? Another way to think about this: when you see someone in your industry doing something that drives you crazy, what is it about their actions, beliefs, or attitudes that make you want to throw something across the room? The answers will begin to reveal your underlying beliefs and values.

Take the time to consider all of the areas of your profession that trigger you or drive you crazy. Get to the bottom of each belief behind that reaction, because they will point you in the direction of what is most important to you.

Step 3: Consider Your Oeuvre
Next, you're going to do a deep dive into your total body of work. Included in your total body of work is all of your accomplishments, professional and otherwise. All of your major projects, your wins and failures, your favorite clients, your best personal stories, the moments in your life that mean a lot to you.

It might be a lot to sift through, but focus on the pieces of your work and life that brought you the most joy and excitement, the pieces that carry the most potential. You may have come to this exercise with a preconceived idea of what you need to create or write. You don't have to abandon that.

What I'm inviting you to do, however, is to widen the scope of what you think is possible and consider how you can look at the best moments in your oeuvre—your total body of work—and bring them into your future work.

Step 4: Decide Who You Will Serve
We already discussed your audience extensively in the last chapter, but think back to the audience exercises you did in the previous chapter. Who are you serving now, and who will you serve through this book? How will your audience change over time? Is it possible you'll be speaking to an entirely different audience in five years? Also, just as we change, so do our clients. Getting clear on this before you move on will help avoid confusion in the future.

Step 5: Reflect on the Confluence of Your Answers
Consider the confluence of the answers. What do you deeply believe? How are you uniquely suited to solve your desired audience's problems, and how does that align with your vision for the next five years? When I work with clients, we look for the thread that lights them up. If the sum total of everything we've gathered feels completely predictable or unexciting—as if you could've guessed exactly where it was going—we need to reconsider. I know we've hit the sweet spot when we discover the nugget that lights my client up—the piece they couldn't see themselves—and gets them excited about where they're going.

Step 6: Find the Process In the Patterns
In this step, you're going to look at the problems your audience faces and consider all the ways that it can be or has been resolved, either by you or by someone else. As you look from all angles, you're looking for patterns.

Keep in mind that the best way to reveal patterns in how a client's or customer's problem gets solved is to have many examples at your disposal. It's okay if you're new to this, and you have only your own personal examples to work from. Your experiences are a perfectly valid place from which to start. It simply points to the need for further testing (which we'll discuss later in the process). If you have few examples to work from, consider the perspectives of other people who have written similar work or have similar stories to yours.

As you work on this step, remember that you want no more than ten major steps to the process—and ten is a stretch. Remember, we have to keep this portable and memorable, and any more than ten steps, rules or principles is too much for anyone to remember. Write them down.

Step 7: Organize Your Ideas
Consider the best order of arrangement so the steps or principles build on top of one another. How do they relate to each other? Organize them in the way that seems most intuitive and allows for the cleanest journey for the reader.

While this may seem straightforward, this can be tricky depending on the topic. For example, you might realize that some audience members might take the steps in a different order if left to their own devices. So which order should it be? It would be easy to get stuck in analysis paralysis, but in the end, you have to decide so you can move forward.

This is one area where intuition, your own gut instinct, will come in handy. As you work, notice what seems right and what doesn't seem to fit, what lights you up and what bores you. Take that into account as you construct your model. In my experience, I know we're going in the right direction when the client feels a sense of excitement about the model they've built. If we don't have that sense of clarity, excitement, and forward momentum, we still have work to do.

Step 8: Test the Framework
Every framework needs to be tested. As I've said, frameworks might not be useful or stand the test of time if they haven't been tested in the real world by real people with real problems.

There are multiple ways to do this, but you want to find a way to test it with people and have them tell you how it worked. Start talking about your framework with people who are in your ideal audience. Watch their reactions. When I first start testing a model, I bring it up in casual conversation and share what I'm working on. Share your framework with a handful of existing clients, ask them to test it, and then ask for the results they get. Look for areas of uncertainty and soft results. You want to make sure it has the same results for people who don't have your experience.

Start writing about your framework, and share it with your audiences. Inevitably, you'll get questions about how it works and people will "poke holes," showing you aspects of the model you hadn't considered. Start testing it in client work where you'll have the opportunity to see the process unfold from a front-row seat.

As you work to test the model, you'll notice that more data brings more and deeper insight. In truth, testing and refining the model could take years (not that you have to wait that long to write the book). It's important to give this step time so you know that you're representing the best solution to the problem for your readers. As you refine, consider:

1. **Originality**: Has what you're saying been said before? "There's nothing new under the sun," so the answer is probably yes, and that's okay. But are you sharing your knowledge in a way that's fresh and uniquely *yours*?

2. **Hidden foundations:** What assumptions is your model based on? What "goes without saying"?

3. **User experience:** How does this model occur to the reader/user/student?

4. **Simplicity vs. Complexity:** How simple or complex is the model?

5. **Applicability:** How is the model implemented?

FINAL THOUGHTS

Your Capstone model is more than an organizing principle—if your book is meant to teach others how to accomplish a goal, it's the foundation everything else will build upon. In the next chapter, we'll explore how to choose the right structural pattern to present this model to your readers, ensuring your hard-earned wisdom reaches them in the most effective way possible.

As you learn about the model and how it acts in the real world, continue to iterate. Your model will likely continue to evolve for a time—over months and years. It may never be done growing and evolving depending on what you teach, so it's okay to think of it as a constant experiment that deserves to be tested and refined. Let it grow and evolve.

chapter six

Choose Your Book's Architecture

Now that you've developed your Capstone model, you need to choose how to present it to your readers. Every successful book follows a clear structural pattern that shapes how information unfolds for the reader. While your Capstone model contains what you'll teach, the structural pattern you choose for your book determines how you'll teach it. Think of this as choosing the right vessel for your message—some ideas are best served by a classic three-act progression, others by a series of interconnected essays, and still others by a hero's journey.

You're already familiar with these structural patterns, even if you've never thought about them consciously. They're present in every book you've read and every movie you've watched. The key is choosing the pattern that will best serve your readers and your message. A well-chosen structure is invisible to the reader but makes your ideas instantly more accessible and memorable.

These patterns aren't rigid formulas or templates—they're flexible blueprints that can be adapted to serve your unique message and audience. These patterns can be used to get you writing and serve you as much as the reader. They might change as you write because you might find your writing has grown and needs another shape to hold it.

In this chapter, we'll explore several proven patterns for organizing your book, from broad architectural frameworks that span entire books to focused structures for individual chapters.

BIG PICTURE PATTERNS

First, let's start with the big picture ideas. The following examples are easiest to see throughout the entire arc of a book. You've likely encountered each one of them before. While they are more often used throughout the entirety of a book, you can also use them in individual chapters.

The 3-Act Structure

The 3-Act Structure is one of the most basic devices in storytelling. You will see this structure played out across movies, plays, television shows… Most of our narratives in Western culture are based on this structure. In fiction, we have the setup, the struggle or confrontation, and the resolution. In nonfiction, we can think of it like this:

Act 1: The introduction of the problem.

Here, we introduce the idea and then explain why the reader should care. We go into depth about the problem and the results of the problem in the reader's life, driving home the idea that they not only should want to fix this problem, but this book or piece of writing will show them how.

Act 2: The solution to the problem.

Over the second act, the writer introduces the reader to the solution.

The reader will learn how to solve the problem using the strategies, stories, and advice in the book. The information is presented in the order that makes the most sense for the reader to absorb and learn from it. Hopefully, the second act can finish with some kind of climax to the information—and that will depend on the content and the creativity of the writer.

Act 3: The resolution.
The third act includes the final details they need to know about implementing the ideas in the book, plus a glimpse of what life will be like once they do. The reader should be left on a positive, inspiring, and uplifting note so they feel ready to take on the strategies the author provided.

The acts can be labeled as "parts" to a book, with the subsequent chapters nested under each part. If you think about organizing your book in this way, think about symmetry. You don't have to have the same number of chapters under each part, but you don't want some parts to be disproportionately larger than other parts.

The Modified 3-Act Structure
In *Tantric Intimacy*, Katrina Bos takes a novel approach to the three-act structure. With five major parts, she sets up with the introduction and then moves right into the beginning of the second act. The reader picks up this book expecting to learn about tantric sex, right? But Katrina's teachings are focused on the idea that tantric intimacy goes absolutely nowhere without one key component: kindness.

Initially, she thought kindness should come at the high point, the climax, of the book. But everything she teaches is built on that idea. Without it, you will never get to the peak of the experience. So, we decided that her book introduces kindness as the foundational principle, while still giving her reader the, ahem, climax they were looking for when they picked up the book (it was too easy, I couldn't help myself). The reader gets what they want, but they also get what they need to make it all work.

Life Lessons & Philosophies
In Ray Dalio's *Principles*, he shares his life story and his tactics for success. The first half of the book is devoted to his life story, while the second half of the book is tactical. Ray doesn't mess around with trying to fuse the two together—he gives the reader the option to turn to the story or turn to the tactics, providing a very clear menu of those tactics in the middle of the book.

However, Ray wasn't a household name when he published the book. He had to provide his life story so the tactics had context. Otherwise, a reader might wonder to themselves, "Why the hell should I listen to this guy?"

In addition to telling his story, he extrapolated the main learning lessons, or the hardship he encountered and overcame, for the major events in his life. His pattern amounts to every third or maybe sixth paragraph containing some explicit, bald-faced nugget of wisdom. It's unnecessary for him to go in-depth—one sentence does enough to tell the reader what he got from that episode of his life and what they might learn from it, too.

There's a lot we can learn from Ray's example. First, splitting the book up into two clear parts makes it easy for the reader to access what they want. Second, outlining a set of principles, or ways to think, makes it easy to organize his writing. Those principles have a hierarchy and a necessary order. Ray only had to think about the order in which his reader needed to learn those principles in order to apply them. His outline was set once he understood the order of his principles.

The Hero's Journey

Another big picture approach is the Hero's Journey. First identified by Joseph Campbell, the Hero's Journey is a mythic structure found in stories all around the world. Most of our famous and beloved cultural stories follow the Hero's Journey. The typical Hero's Journey has twelve main stages, with a few finer points scattered between stages. The main stages include:

- **Ordinary World:** life as it is before the hero is called to the journey
- **Call to Adventure:** the compelling moment where it's clear the hero must leave his or her comfortable world and heed the call
- **Meeting the Mentor:** the first guide who helps them on their way
- **Crossing the Threshold into the New World:** finally heeding the call to adventure
- **Test, Allies, and Enemies:** the hero meets still more mentors and enemies and undergoes a series of tests that they have to pass before attempting the real test
- **Approach to Inmost Cave:** the big test
- **Ordeal, Death, and Rebirth:** the all is lost moment
- **Reward (Seizing the Sword):** the hero has faced down death and retrieves the reward, which can be intrinsic or extrinsic
- **The Road Back:** the hero begins the return home with the sword or the elixir of life that they earned in their trials
- **Resurrection:** the hero faces the final confrontation with the enemy
- **Return with Elixir:** the hero finally returns home with the rewards of their journey

There are two ways to approach this in a nonfiction book. First, if you have quite a lot of narrative, it's fairly intuitive to arrange the stories so they follow this clear arc. Second, consider thinking of your reader as the hero. This makes organizing your book a little easier if you know which stage of the ordeal they need to go through in each chapter. There are all kinds of variations on this theme, and when you do it right, readers will easily resonate with it.

The Collection of Essays

In *You Are a Badass*, Jen Sincero shares her wisdom in a series of engaging and funny essays. Each essay is short, to the point, and only as long as it needs to be to get the reader to understand what she's saying. Then, she extrapolates the major lessons from the story and shares them with the reader in numbered or bulleted points.

Rather than follow a time-oriented narrative arc, she follows an editorial arc. Meaning, her stories aren't sequential. The stories are only there as the gateway to her main point. The chapters are organized around her main point, what the reader needs to "get" first, and then second, and then third, and the stories are matched to the point. To use this frame, you could write out each of your main thoughts on one sheet of paper, one sentence each. Then build each chapter around the main thought using a story as the entry point for the reader.

The Collection of Thoughts

Writer Steven Pressfield takes the collection of essays and makes it even simpler. In his classics *The Authentic Swing*, *The War of Art*, and *The Artist's Journey*, he writes each main idea as simply as possible. Some of his essays are three pages long and some are just one sentence. Each chapter is headed with his main point, the takeaway he wants you to have.

He blends historical references and personal anecdotes and never writes more than what he needs to make the point. This is the kind of soundbite writing people love and gravitate towards because it's so well-written (counterintuitively, simple writing is the hardest) and because it's so digestible. Anyone can pick this book up, turn to any page, and get something from it without needing to know what came before or after.

THE SMALLER PICTURE

Next, we're going to look at some more specific ways of writing using patterns. These are normally used on a chapter-level basis.

The Persuasive Argument

In Sheryl Sandberg's *Lean In*, she and her co-author have a rough template that they use throughout the book. Since she is trying to persuade and teach about the challenges and barriers women face in the workplace and how to overcome them, she opens each chapter with an illustrative story or research and then dives into her supporting points. If you take out the first and sometimes the last sentence of each paragraph in the chapter, you can see the complete argument she's making. The rough outline of each chapter looks like this:

- Illustrative story
    - Main point of the chapter
        - Supporting point 1
        - Supporting point 2
        - Supporting point 3
        - Supporting point 4
        - Supporting point 5
- Illustrative story
    - Second major point of the chapter
        - Supporting point 1

- Supporting point 2
  - Supporting point 3
  - Supporting point 4
  - Supporting point 5
- Concluding thoughts of chapter, bringing in each of the major points

Each supporting point could be a piece of research, an experience, a personal story, a historical story, etc. In *Lean In*, each supporting point can be seen at the beginning or end of the paragraph in which it is written. This works best when you are persuading readers of a belief or an argument and pulling in a lot of different pieces of information to support your points. Sitting down to write out your thoughts and then diving deep on the major underlying principles of your belief is a good way to flesh out what you're trying to say.

The Funnel
This is best for chapters where you have one main idea, several points to make about it, and then tactical information. What makes these chapters tricky is that it's often hard to discern which tactics are most important to the reader and which order they should be arranged in the chapter.

With the funnel, you start with the most important idea at the top. This is your main point, the thing you really want them to understand. Think of it like this: If your reader decides to skim the book and each chapter, what one point would you want them to learn from each chapter? Then, provide the next most important point after, and so on.

The next two sections are more than likely a story, research, or a persuasive argument to convince the reader why your main point is important. All of your tactics should follow in that order, ending with the least significant. With this organization, your reader can return to the chapter and use it as a reference, knowing what they can expect because they read it in the first few sections.

IN CLOSING

The structural pattern you've chosen will serve as the architecture for your book, giving shape to your Capstone model (if you're using one) and making your message more accessible to readers. I encourage you to try on some patterns of your own. There are dozens more beyond what I've shared here. I also encourage you to go back to your favorite books and see if you can find the patterns hidden within them. However you decide to use these, please remember that a pattern or template is no replacement for creativity. Use the pattern, but shape it to your own needs.

Now it's time to create the detailed roadmap that will guide your writing process—your outline. In the next chapter, we'll explore how to develop an outline that works with your natural writing style while keeping your book focused and effective.

chapter seven

Build Your Outline

Now that you've developed your Capstone model and chosen the structural pattern to present it, it's time to create your detailed writing plan. Many writers cringe at the word "outline," seeing it as a creativity-killing constraint. But a good outline isn't a cage—it's a map that helps you navigate from your initial idea to a finished book. In this chapter, we'll explore different approaches to outlining that work with your natural writing style while keeping your book focused and purposeful.

Outlining has a bad rap. The word "outlining" is so unsexy that it makes your fingers curl away from the keyboard in disgust. It reminds us of our grade school days when we had to painstakingly create an outline for a paper that we didn't want to write in the first place. But it doesn't have to be such a drag.

You're clear on why you're writing the book, who you're writing it for, and what you have to share. Hopefully, you feel enthusiastic about what you've put together so far, and if that's the case, outlining might not be so bad. It might even be… exciting.

This is the stage where you get to brainstorm, ideate, write down all of your good, crazy, out-there ideas, and set them up next to each other to decide what stays and what goes. That can be a lot of fun.

Outlines can be one page long or thirty pages long. It all depends on what you need as a writer, which brings me to my first and most crucial advice about outlines. Very structured, detailed outlines usually work well for an analytical thinker who needs a roadmap, and they move quickly because the outline tells them exactly what to write next. On the other hand, intuitive writers know their topic but they have no idea what will come out when they write—and they like it that way. They are certainly capable of being analytical, but in their creative process, they lean toward a looser process and rely on their intuition. What comes out as they write is as much a surprise to themselves as it is to anyone else.

For those intuitive writers, outlining a book or any other piece of writing will make them feel as if they're stifled. In fact, writing a detailed outline is almost a waste of time because they probably won't follow it anyway. They need to feel their way through the process. I happen to speak from experience when I say this can be a challenge.

In my work with clients, I am analytical and like to work from a detailed outline. In my own creative work, I'm far more intuitive. This is where my most creative work is written, but intuitive writers tend to have the hardest time making sense of their work when it's finished. Not in the sense that "the words don't make sense," but we tend to have a dozen stories and essays that read well on the page but might not have an obvious thread running through them. This usually means we need more time to sort things out on the back end.

If you're an intuitive writer, you might be better off focusing on a scoped-out, high-level outline that captures the major themes, parts, and chapters of the book and some of the associated ideas rather than planning and outlining in detail. By focusing on the general theme of each chapter, you'll be giving yourself enough room to explore and move without feeling constricted.

Understanding where you fall on the spectrum of analytical or intuitive is not for the purpose of changing that about yourself. I encourage you to avoid fighting against your creative nature and allow yourself to outline and write in the way that works for you, even if it looks vastly different from the way everyone else does it. Trying to be analytical when you are intuitive (and vice versa) is like pouring water on a fire… you'll snuff your creative heat. Don't force yourself into being creative in a way that doesn't work for you.

The second crucial bit of advice about outlines is that they are not static, meaning no outline is set in stone. Outlines change, rearrange, and expand as the book project progresses. This seems obvious, and yet first-time writers and authors feel like they owe the original outline loyalty or that it should serve as some kind of map that never changes. So, they refuse to reconsider the outline, even when circumstances call for it. Inevitably, the outline of the book you finish is going to look different from the outline you started with. Relax your grip on your outline, and you'll be able to see and sense when the flow of the book needs to change.

The directions below are based on a few assumptions: you're writing a nonfiction book, and you have several years (or decades) of experience or stories to share. Whether you are intuitive or analytical, treat your outline like part of your roadmap on your creative journey. The clearer the roadmap, the smoother the journey.

There are two components to a good outline: getting clear on your content (you've done a lot of that work in the previous chapters) and getting a grasp on the ideal order and flow of that content so your reader enjoys the journey. Below, I'll share three methods for creating your outline.

METHOD ONE: USE YOUR CAPSTONE MODEL

In Chapter 6, we went over the process for identifying the mental models and philosophies that support your work. If you went through the exercises in that chapter, you can use your framework as the basis of your outline. You'll need to consider the following:

1. What kind of introductory conversation do I need to have with my readers? What questions do they usually have when they first encounter my work?

2. How can I help them understand the problem they're experiencing (and looking to solve) better than they do right now?

3. Does each step in the process or each philosophy get its own chapter? Section?

4. What other information does the reader need to have to be able to use my model to the fullest degree possible?

Most readers need some kind of entry point so they can feel connected to what the writer is saying, and so they can identify themselves as someone who will benefit from the book. Let's say you have a four-step Capstone model that you'll be sharing in your book. You would set up the outline by first talking about the problem. Then you'd present the solution. Then you'd present some scenarios and use case examples that help the reader understand how to use the model. So, the outline might look like this:

- Introduction
- Chapter 1: Current State of Affairs: what their world is like now, and why the problem exists

- Chapter 2: What they don't know about the problem
- Chapter 3: How the problem is affecting them
- Chapter 4: Introduction and Explanation of the Capstone Model
- Chapter 5: Step 1
- Chapter 6: Step 2
- Chapter 7: Step 3
- Chapter 8: Step 4
- Chapter 9: How to use the Capstone Model, as well as case studies and examples of others who have used it
- Chapter 10: Growing beyond this stage...[?]
- Conclusion

This is a very simple, high-level outline with which to start. If the writer of this outline wanted more detail, they could flesh it out like this:

- Introduction
  - Opening story: best example of a client success story
  - Set authority: explain how you came to be an expert in this field
  - Promise: share the promise to the reader (which we talked about in Chapter 5)
- Chapter 1: Current State of Affairs: what their world is like now, and why the problem exists
  - Description of where they're at (show you understand them and their problem)
  - Share reason #1 that the problem exists
  - Share reason #2 that the problem exists
  - Share reason #3 that the problem exists
- Chapter 2: What they don't know about the problem
  - Case study that exemplifies the hidden factors to the problem

- Hidden factor #1
  - Hidden factor #2
  - Hidden factor #3
- Chapter 3: How the problem is affecting them
  - Share what happens when the problem doesn't get fixed
  - Share the future vision of the ongoing problem
- Chapter 4: Introduction and Explanation of the Capstone Model
  - Share the model and give a brief overview of each step
- Chapter 5: Step 1
  - Go in-depth on Step 1
- Chapter 6: Step 2
  - Go in-depth on Step 2
- Chapter 7: Step 3
  - Go in-depth on Step 3
- Chapter 8: Step 4
  - Go in-depth on Step 4
- Chapter 9: How to use the Capstone Model, as well as case studies and examples of others who have used it
- Share one case study/example of someone who has used the model successfully
  - Extrapolate what they did and explain why it worked
  - Give tips to the reader so they can implement it in their world
- Chapter 10: Growing beyond this stage…[?]
  - Share story of someone who is 2-3 steps beyond where the reader is now
  - Share tips for growing beyond the model
- Conclusion

This is simply a template, not a strict recommendation. You can take elements of this outline and create one that works for you. (You can also find a downloadable template for this outline at sarastibitz.

com) The point is to use your framework as the basis for the content in your outline, and then use the introductory paragraphs to set up why they need the model and the conclusory paragraphs to help them understand all the ways they can apply it.

METHOD TWO: BRAINSTORM

If you aren't using a mental model or framework in your book, you can use another method to pull your ideas together. First, you'll inventory your knowledge, thoughts, and ideas. Then you'll reflect, refine and research.

Step One: Inventory Your Knowledge, Thoughts, & Ideas

First, decide what tool works best for you, and then you're going to write down all of the ideas that you have that relate to the premise and promise of your book. Every single one of them.

This is the point in the process where you remove any mental barriers that stop you from ideating. You can get messy, crazy, creative, out-there, downright weird—you're going to write it all down, even if you know it may not end up in the book. You're going to write down both the ideas you're dying to talk about and the ideas that bore you to death but are important to your subject. Your inner critic or cynic should be turned off so you can consider every idea that walks in the door.

There are a couple of methods you can use to approach this activity:

- **Post-its:** You can keep it simple and have one color or use different colors to differentiate between chapters, ideas, steps, or topics. Jot down one idea/note per post-it. You can keep them in a pile, or better yet, find a poster board to stick them to so you can see them all laid out. This makes them easier to rearrange later.

- **Word processor:** Popular options include Google Docs, Microsoft Word, or Scrivener. If you prefer to go old school, use Microsoft Word to start, although collaboration can get messy down the road. If you intend to share this outline or the work with anyone, I recommend Google Docs simply because it makes collaboration much easier. Scrivener is wonderful but has a steep learning curve. As of this writing, docs in Scrivener aren't shareable, so collaboration is more of a challenge.
- **Pen and paper:** There is nothing like physically writing down your thoughts. Writing down your idea helps you get a hold of what you're going to write about. You can use lists, bubbles, bullet points, mind maps, or whatever works for you.
- **Whiteboard:** Everyone loves a good whiteboard session. Grab a marker, and start jotting things down.
- **Mindmeister.com (or a similar software):** This is a wonderful online whiteboard and mind-mapping tool. There are multiple ways to set up the view so your work can evolve as you narrow down your subjects and ideas.
- **Evernote:** Some people love the simplicity of Evernote's ability to store a variety of media—notes, recordings, articles, books, etc. This is a good route to take if you already have your notes or research saved on this platform.

There is no wrong way to do this—the right way is the way that gets it done for you. I find that writing things down with a pen or marker in hand tends to be more creatively inspiring and fun. The tangible experience of writing as the ideas take shape is far more rewarding than the feel of keys under my fingers at this stage. Plus, it gets me out of my headspace and into an embodied creative process. If you like having things in digital format, don't worry—you'll move it online after the messy part is over.

I also recommend getting out of your normal comfort zone when you brainstorm. If you work in the same space every day, go outside, to a bookstore or coffee shop, or someplace that inspires you. A fellow writer likes to go to Las Vegas every time he starts a new book. He finds the novel environment to be creatively inspiring and far different from his home. Being in a new environment stimulates you in new ways and helps you generate new ideas or connections between ideas.

Keep in mind that ideating might take several sessions. You might think you have it all down, and then as soon as you walk away from it, a new idea will take root, or you'll remember something you want to include. Let the process unfold over a few days, and be sure to carry a notepad with you so you can quickly capture your ideas as they come up. Leave no idea unrecorded!

Step Two: Reflect and Refine
Once you've gathered all of the possible ideas you have about your premise, give yourself a few days to let them sit. Don't rush this part.

In *A Technique for Producing Ideas*, author James Webb Young writes that after gathering all of the information available to us and studying it, we must then step away and let the subconscious mind work on the material we've collected. When the time is right, the project will return to you with a flash of insight and clarity. Not that I recommend waiting until you have total clarity, but I trust you to know when the time is right to return to the results of your work. By the time you revisit this, you will likely have some clarity about the direction your book will take.

When I first return to my ideas, I like to look at those that kept nagging at me over the previous few days. I'm also searching for the main points I want to make in the book. Look for the ideas that excite you and bore you, and look for those that truly emphasize your premise and underscore the solution or way of thinking that you're giving your readers.

Start by cutting out everything you don't think you need to cover: physically take them out of your pile of post-its or remove the ideas from the list. This could include tangents or topics that are so far outside of the scope of what the reader needs that it might be a distraction.

Don't throw them out or delete them altogether, though; you might need to refer to them later. Just put them aside and out of the way for now. I like to create a document or a separate notebook in Evernote and label it "Parking lot for [title of book]." This lets you set these ideas down someplace without losing them because they could be the seeds for your next book.

Next, identify the ideas that are so obviously necessary or intrinsic to the topic you're discussing. These are the main ideas you'll present in your book, the ones the reader can't possibly skip. In other words, for your reader to follow your argument or what you're teaching, they *must* understand these topics. They might be the topics that bore you the most or the ones you assume they already know. This might be an exploration of the problem or the solutions that haven't worked in the past. Don't assume; make sure you're carefully considering the book from the perspective of your reader (and if this means polling some ideal readers to ask them, then do it).

Look for the natural order that might arise from your ideas. Think about how the reader might need to encounter the information for them to truly understand it. Is there a hierarchy to the pieces or a way in which they must flow and build on one another? Do you have to teach one topic before you can introduce another topic?

As you work, think about how the ideas and topics flow into chapters. Are some topics big enough to warrant a full chapter? Or are some topics so big that they take up almost an entire "part" of the book? Are some topics important but not enough to fill a full chapter? What ideas correspond to those topics?

At this point, you probably have some kind of order for topics and ideas, and maybe even an emerging Table of Contents. Most likely, many of the remaining ideas that have not found a home are subsets of the main topics you've already arranged—or they're not necessary. Go through each remaining idea and determine where it fits relative to your main topics. Use the same sequential order here: If the reader needs to understand a particular subtopic to fully understand another subtopic, then put them in order.

If you're having trouble placing any of the ideas from your pile, it may be that they're tangential to the overall topic or too far into the weeds for you to cover in this book. Remember, your book will need to reach the reader you identified earlier in the process. The reader might not need expert-level advice that would only intimidate or distract them. Save that idea for your next book.

After completing this process, add any leftover ideas to the Parking Lot document. Turning back to the outline, take stock of what you see. Does each main topic or idea have a balanced number of supporting points? You may notice that you have ten subtopics under one topic but only one or two subtopics under another. You may need to cull some of the subtopics and include only those that are essential or reevaluate each one to see if it nests where you initially put it.

Next, look at your main points and subtopics. Are there stories that immediately come to mind that would illustrate your topic? Do you have case studies from clients you've worked with? Is there research that could fill in and support the idea? How about images or graphs? Make notes where you will include those supporting pieces of information.

A note on stories, research, and the like: If you're going to use them, you want to have a nice mix of each spread throughout the book. If you don't have them now, you can find them when you do further research. You don't need to tell a story every time you introduce a fresh topic, nor do you need new research. The last thing you want is a book that is so formulaic and predictable that the reader gets bored.

Consider the topic and how the idea can best be conveyed to the reader. If the topic requires the emotional engagement of a reader, then a story might be the best way to start. If a topic you're introducing is so counterintuitive and surprising that your reader will question the truth of it, then you might want to start with research or anecdotal experience.

Step Three: Research

When we've been immersed in a topic for any length of time, it's easy to tell ourselves that we know everything there is to know. And we're wrong about that—there are always new ideas to consider, updated research studies, and philosophies to revisit. Writing a book is a great way to deepen your knowledge of your field.

Your outline probably contains points and ideas that you know very well and could teach at the drop of a hat. It's equally likely that your outline includes ideas that need new or updated research. Start with the topics for which you have little information. Consider what you've said or written about them before. Have you been able to avoid going in-depth on these topics because your ideal reader or client usually has the baseline knowledge they need to understand your teachings? If you have taught this topic, what did you say in the past, and what can you add now in your book? Chances are, you know where your teachings or ideas are weak, so begin your research there.

If you have chosen to self-publish, there is no one standing over your shoulder forcing you to cite your sources or back your ideas. But I strongly recommend that you do the work of giving credit to your sources. It boosts your credibility with the reader, and it maintains the integrity of what you're saying—the reader knows that you've done your homework and that you know what you're talking about. Plus, you're giving credit where it is due. In an age where anyone can say anything online, this is increasingly more important. We need to acknowledge that we stand on the shoulders of giants.

As you research, make sure you track your sources. Tracking your research sources as you go makes it infinitely easier when it comes time to add citations to your book later—you don't have to hunt down that URL or source. Personally, I like Zotero, which is free and downloadable software that can be used to track your sources, but there are dozens of other options available.

As you work, add each bit of new information to your outline. If you are creating a detailed outline, drill down on each topic, subtopic, and supporting point and idea as much as you can. Look at every given topic and follow each open question that arises until no further questions arise—keep going until you've got an outline that gives you the confidence to get started. This is a subjective standard—some writers need a lot of detail to feel ready, while others just need to know what they're talking about in the next chapter. You want to have enough of an outline to give you a roadmap and to remove any doubt as to what you're writing, but there's no need to strive for perfection.

METHOD THREE: THE RETROSPECTIVE OUTLINE
The previous two outlines assume that you decided to write a book and set out to do it in a (somewhat) organized fashion. But that's

not how all books get written. Just as often, a writer will come to me with tons of content that they've written over the years with the desire to pull it together into a book. So, this method is for those who are starting with a whole lot of content and want to know how to pull it together into a book.

A couple of notes here. Having a lot of content does not mean you have a book. I see this frequently with podcasters, bloggers, and folks who have a lot of course material; they believe that somehow, some way, everything will amount to a full-length written work. This is a wonderful place from which to start, but you have to understand that a book is a completely different format from short-form or spoken content and requires a cohesive premise to pull it all together. Often, when authors get specific and clear about the premise, they realize that a good portion of the content they have doesn't work, and then they feel discouraged about the amount of writing they have to do. This is a perfectly normal place to start. Just don't let it catch you by surprise.

Also, when considering an outline for material you already have in hand, don't let the tail wag the dog. In other words, the writing you have shouldn't dictate the book. Don't create an outline or structure that distorts itself just to include existing content. Set the writing aside and consider the outline from the perspective of what's absolutely necessary and important to support the premise of the book.

Review

The first step in this process is to review the content you have. This might seem like an obvious first step, and yet so many would-be authors avoid it. They do this for a few reasons: they have so much content that the thought of going through all of it is intimidating or off-putting; they have a fear (often unspoken) that the content they have isn't all that good, doesn't apply to the book they want to write, or is outdated and needs a lot of updating; their content is so unorganized that it's difficult to read through. As a result, they avoid the task of actually reading through their previous work to get a better understanding of where they stand.

There's no skipping this step. It will be next to impossible to create a cohesive outline for your content if you don't know the content you have.

So, knowing that, best practices include:

1. **Give yourself ample time.** Only you know how much content you have and what your schedule allows, so give yourself a generous amount of time to review your material. For example, if you have years of podcast interviews to comb through, a couple of hours on a Saturday afternoon isn't going to cut it.

2. **Notice the themes that arise.** There are definitely themes to your work. You might already know some of them, but your deep dive into your work might reveal other themes that you didn't notice were there. Jot these down so you can track some of the major ideas, topics, and themes that may serve as the organizing principles for your book.

3. **Organize as you go.** You might already have your content well organized, but chances are it's a little chaotic. As you comb through, find a way to label, tag, or put into folders each piece of content. You may not know how it all fits into an outline as you organize, but you will see pieces that are related to one another. Consider using Evernote or Notion to track your work. Both apps make it easy to tag and organize content so you can search and find it later.

4. Decide what doesn't go in. As you read, you will notice that some pieces don't seem to fit the premise of your book. Put those aside and label them in a way that you can find them later if needed.

5. Notice what's missing. What areas are thin on content or non-existent? What topics do you skim over, and in what areas do you go deep? Notice areas that may need more attention or work to provide the depth your readers will need.

As you approach this, remember that, while we are linear readers, we are not always linear writers. Your written work might have evolved organically but will need to be reconsidered from the point of the reader. You'll have to ask yourself: in what order does the reader need to encounter the information to make it easy for them to grasp?

Reflect

After you've combed through all of your existing content, take some time to reflect on what you've just read. What major themes show up in your work? Where are you drowning in content, and where is the content lacking? What do you have to offer readers?

Usually, after a writer does a review of their work, they either know that they're ready to put the pieces of their book together and expand on the writing, or they come to the clear-eyed decision that they are not quite ready for that step, and their ideas need more development. Only you can decide in which camp you fall.

If you decide that you're ready to assemble what you have into a draft and continue to write, then go to the previous outlining method (Method 2), and begin there.

USING YOUR OUTLINE AS YOU WRITE

Remember, your outline is a living document that will grow and change as you write. You will likely change the way you think about your book (and your topic) as you write, perhaps many times. Use your Capstone model, chosen structure, and outline as tools to serve you and your readers—not rigid constraints. As you move forward into the writing process, keep referring back to these three elements: your Capstone model shows what to teach, your structural pattern shows how to present it, and your outline shows the path forward. Together, they form the foundation for a book that will effectively share your knowledge with the world.

PART 3

BREAKING GROUND

The act of writing is more than simply putting thoughts to the page; it is just as much about managing your thoughts and emotions as it is about choosing your words. No amount of structure, strategy, or technique will matter if you're constantly at war with your own mind. This part of the book is dedicated to you, the writer, and the emotional and logistical realities that come with this work.

Every writer faces resistance—fear, doubt, procrastination, perfectionism—the unseen forces that can grind progress to a halt. But mastery doesn't mean eliminating these forces; it means learning to work with them. It means understanding your own creative rhythms, building systems that support you, and navigating the inevitable self-doubt with compassion and clarity.

In these two chapters, we'll explore both the emotional landscape of writing and the practical systems that keep you moving forward. Whether you're battling the inner critic, trying to establish a consistent routine, or wondering how to stay motivated when inspiration runs dry, this section will offer insight, strategies, and reassurance. Writing is more than a creative act—it's an act of self-leadership.

chapter eight

Create Your Writing Plan

Before you launch into writing, you must create a writing plan that sets you up for success. How do we do that? By first understanding what kind of writing plan will set you up for failure.

The greatest mistake you can make is to set yourself an unreasonable goal or deadline. It's not uncommon for an author to request help with editing one month out from the book launch date they publicly declared on all of their social media channels. Or they might tell me that they have an arrangement with a publisher and a submission deadline that's fast approaching—and not one word has been written. This happens because of a combination of enthusiasm, impatience, and total ignorance as to what it takes to get a book from concept to physical product. Deadlines are important, but they're not the place to start.

STEP 1: GET A GRIP ON YOUR TIME AND HABITS
There are two important pieces to grasp here: The existing time you have available for writing in your already-packed schedule, and how long it takes you to write a certain amount of words.

Let's talk about your schedule first. Most first-time authors set a writing schedule or a goal without ever truly looking at their calendars to see how much time they have available for this endeavor. If you're reading this book, you are likely a busy entrepreneur or career-oriented professional. You most likely have a family, and you spend a lot of time with them. You probably exercise and have some hobbies or practices that mean a lot to your well-being. A healthy writing habit should honor all of the things in your life that you already hold dear... meaning, you shouldn't have to cut out or forgo anything that's truly important to you.

You will have to make or find time, however. Look at your calendar and take into account all of the following:

- Daily or weekly set open times that are available for writing
- Daily or weekly set meetings or commitments
- Upcoming holidays or vacations over the next six months that will take time or interrupt a writing schedule
- Unscheduled time... for example, if you are a caretaker of children or parents, you likely don't have your time with them scheduled on the calendar. Figure out how much time those caretaking activities take per week
- Low-interest or low-stakes activities you could cancel or reschedule to make room for writing

Many of us go into this exercise thinking we're going to have lots of time to write, only to look at our actual lives and what's planned for the next six months and realize that we're going to be lucky if we get three to five hours a week—or less. That might be sobering, but it's better to start with a realistic idea of the time you actually have available to you, rather than an ideal that's not based on reality. Setting writing goals that are misaligned with reality only sets you up for failure right out of the gate.

As you consider what to cut or move, don't scrap the things that keep you healthy and happy, like a morning exercise habit or meditation routine. It may seem like a good idea to sacrifice these activities for your writing in the short term. The problem with that thinking arises from the fact that writing a book is not a "short" process. You're only hurting yourself in the long run, and you'd be taking away the activities that support you and your creative process.

Next, consider what time you might have available to schedule writing sprints. Scheduling a week-long or weekend writing sprint several times in the months ahead can give you something to look forward to and help move your book along at a much faster pace.

Also, think about what it's like for you to write:

- When is your best creative time? Are you more generative and clear in the morning, afternoon, or evening?
- When do you like to write, versus when do you like to think or ideate?
- How long does it take you to get warmed up?
- What gets in the way of your writing?

When you think about the time you're going to allot for writing, take all of these answers into consideration.

By the end of this exercise, you should have a clear idea of how many hours you have available to you every week or month, and where those hours fall on the calendar. For example, a client of mine is a Night Owl and likes to write when her family goes to bed. Her available time looks like this:

> Monday: 9 - 11 PM
> Thursday: 9 - 11 PM
> Saturday: 9 - 12 AM

This Night Owl has a total of seven hours per week to work with, and she plans to add one weekend writing sprint per month. Or consider another client, whose schedule is far more difficult between juggling his business and his family life. He can only wedge time in early in the morning:

> Tuesday: 6 - 8 AM
> Friday: 6 - 8 AM

This Early Bird has a total of four hours per week to work with. If he can schedule a week-long writing sprint, he'll be giving himself a big boost in available time.

Now let's consider my friend, the Erratic Magpie, who doesn't like to operate by a schedule. She doesn't like to be told exactly when to write—she wants to write when the inspiration strikes. The idea of a writing plan makes her skin crawl just a little, but she knows that she hasn't been able to get it done by shooting from the hip. It takes her a little longer to finish things because they need to marinate. She needs some kind of plan to keep her on track, or she'll get nowhere.

This is me. I'm talking about me—at least when it comes to my own creative work.

Jokes aside, I am not alone. Although a daily writing plan looks and sounds good, a vast number of my creative friends out there like to write when they feel inspired to write. While there are plenty of quotes out there from writers who are absolutely (almost smugly) certain that a consistent, daily, hours-long writing schedule is the only way to get good at writing, I beg to differ. It just doesn't work for everyone. And that's totally okay, but you're here because you want to write a book, and I'm going to tell you that you still need some kind of rough plan to keep you moving, or you will stall out.

If this is you, consider setting a rough weekly goal, to be accomplished whenever the mood strikes. Some writers decide to set a goal of four hours per week, and they might hit that goal in one streak on a Tuesday afternoon or eke it out in 30-minute stints of free time. How you accomplish your goal might differ wildly week by week, but it's setting the goal that matters.

However, this does not absolve you from planning out your week and putting your writing time in your schedule. Without that step, you're not likely to find the time to write.

STEP 2: CONSIDER YOUR WRITING SPEED
The next thing to consider is how quickly and how well you write. It can be tough to get this measure, especially if you're just building a writing habit. It can be difficult to gauge how much work you can get done during each writing session. But we're going to try, so you have a rough approximation of how long it will take you to write your book.

There are a couple of ways to gauge how much writing you get done in a given time. The first is to time yourself the next time you write an article or blog post. See how long it takes you to get from idea to rough draft.

You'll need a few different samples—the speed of your writing is going to be dependent on the clarity of your thought. When you know what to say, writing goes faster. When you're figuring it out as you go, you will write slower.

Another way to figure out writing speed is to try a timed writing test and learn your "word per minute" rate, something that's easily findable online. You can try 1, 3, and 5-minute tests that will give you your words per minute rate, as well as your error rate.

The average typing speed is 40 words per minute. If we say we have 60 minutes to write, and we write consistently at about the same speed, then it's possible that we could write up to 2400 words in an hour. But wait! That time doesn't account for the time we need to pause and take a sip of tea or coffee, to find that research or that note we made in another app, or to use the restroom, or to stare out the window while we figure something out. It also doesn't take into account the clarity the writer does or doesn't have about what they're writing. It's an upper-limit possibility that we can consider, but it's not the likely outcome of an hour spent at the keyboard.

So, if we take into account the reality of being human, let's just say that for someone with a typing speed of at least 40 words per minute, an hour's worth of writing could generate between 1000 and 2000 words.

For those who plan on speaking out the rough draft of their book, i.e. using dictation software, you're going to have to add in the step of first speaking through your outline and chapters, and then working with the transcript to turn it into a rough draft (a transcript alone is not a rough draft). Some questions when considering how much time it will take:

- Have you presented your topic often? People who've had to teach their topic in front of an audience usually have an easier time with dictation than others.
- How clear are you about your topic? Do you have to stop and start to figure out what you want to say?
- How do you get your point across? Are you clear and straightforward, or are you a circular story-teller who has to take two steps forward and one step back when telling a story or explaining

something? The latter will take a little more time, and will create more work when you start to refine the draft.

A word of caution here: At this point, we're only looking at the potential for words generated so we can get a vague idea of how long it will take you to write your rough draft. But you should know that 1000 words per hour do not automatically equate to 1000 *good* words that are usable for a final draft. As prolific author Neil Gaiman said:

> A good day is defined by anything more than 1,500 words of comfortable, easy writing that I figure I'm probably going to use most of in the end. Occasionally, you have those magical days when you look up and you've done 4,000 words, but they're more than balanced out by those evil days where you manage 150 words you know you'll be throwing away.[5]

As you think about setting a general word count goal for your work sessions, think about who you really are as a writer and creator, not just who you want to be. Setting a goal based on the way you actually write will go so much farther than setting a goal based on an ideal.

STEP 3: CREATE A SCHEDULE

Next, you're going to take a calendar and map out the prospective time it will take you to write your book.

But first, we need to sidestep for a moment and talk about size. Because size doesn't matter. It's what you do with it that counts. Size of the book, I mean. Get your mind out of the gutter.

You'd be surprised how often someone asks some variation of the following question: "How many pages until it's a 'real' book?" This question assumes that the book is not "real" if it doesn't have a certain page count or thickness. That it won't be taken seriously or have an impact if it's short. That one must diligently work to add content—whether the work actually needs more words or not—to get it to the "right" size to achieve "real book" status.

This is the part where I unashamedly beg you to put those thoughts aside. Bookshelves everywhere are becoming increasingly lined with glorified 20,000-word essays—with clear, strong, insightful ideas—that have been padded by an extra 40,000 words to meet the industry standard of what makes a full-length book. This needs to change.

What makes a book is not its length but its depth, portability, and design.

Once authors are freed from the idea that they need to hit a prescribed word count to be taken seriously, their books typically fall somewhere in the 40,000 to 55,000-word range. Some write even shorter books in the 30,000-word range, knowing that they want to deliver their message quickly and spend no more time doing it than necessary.

Let's assume our Night Owl author wants to write a 40,000-word book. She has seven hours per week to write. She thinks she can write about 1200 words per hour. That would give her the potential to write 8400 words per week. If she actually reached her word count, she could have a rough draft in about five weeks, assuming there are no holidays, vacations, or other major interruptions to her schedule.

The Early Bird author has only four hours a week to work with, and he's pretty sure he can only write about 1000 words per hour. That gives him 4000 words per week. He thinks he has enough content that he will end up with a 60,000-word draft. This puts him at 15 weeks until he has a complete rough draft, or a little over three months, assuming there are no holidays, vacations, or other major interruptions to his schedule.

Figure out your rough goal—the approximate word count that you're going for. Then, do the math to figure out how long it would take you given your time available and your writing speed. Understand two things: this is just a rough approximation of how long it will take to write your book based on your prospective word-count and writing speed; and this does not include the time you'll need for revision.

Next, look at your calendar. Notice that I wrote the following phrase for both Night Owl and Early Bird: "assuming there are no holidays, vacations, or other major interruptions to his schedule." Friend, there are always interruptions to the schedule. *Always.* Instead of pretending that they won't happen, or that nothing can get in your way, schedule the interruptions into your writing plan as best you can. Don't force yourself into writing through every single holiday, family vacation, or major undertaking you may have looming on the horizon unless there's a very good reason for it (and the only real reason that has weight is that you have a contractual deadline with a publisher). This is a good way to burn yourself out and cause you to resent your book.

Also, take into account your lifestyle and your cycles of work and rest. I can get about 1500 to 2000 words written in an hour if I know what I'm saying. That's pretty good. But I also know that at certain points during the month, I have low energy. During that time, there will be days when I will show up for my scheduled writing time and be in no place to generate or create. So, I might plan to read books that are related to what I'm writing or do research instead, which helps me maintain a practice of engaging with the book on a regular basis.

Taking into account all of the possible interruptions, map out your writing plan by actually writing in the possible word count and scheduling your work sessions into your calendar.

STEP 4: TRACK YOUR PROGRESS

As you write, you're going to want to track your progress so that you can both understand where you are in the process of writing your rough draft and accommodate your writing plan as you learn more about the way you work.

There are plenty of apps that help you track word count, but you can also keep it super simple by tracking word count in a spreadsheet. Whatever you use needs to be easy for you to update and see your progress. It's the visibility of progress that helps keep you on track and moving toward your goals.

As you track, revisit your writing plan. Within the first few weeks, you'll notice what's working and what's not working. Like your outline, your writing plan has to adjust to real life. Use what you learn to adjust the word count goal and the writing hours you schedule for yourself.

Remember that, throughout the process, you're going to learn what it takes to get into flow, to get into a rhythm that works with your lifestyle and your schedule. The point is to start out with a rough idea of how much time you have available and, given that constraint, how long it could take you to write your book.

STEP 5: CONSIDER YOUR FUTURE EDITOR

Most authors complete their book and then think about hiring an editor. This is a bad move for a number of reasons. First, you'll want time to do revisions, which we'll discuss in Chapter 10. Second, if you want to keep the book moving without any lag time, you'll need to consider the schedule of your prospective editor (I'm speaking directly to those who will self-publish). Start reaching out to prospective editors about a month before you finish your rough draft. Some editors have waiting lists, and you'll want to get on their schedule early. This also conveniently serves as an external deadline that will help motivate you to do your work.

Think about getting your editor on board even earlier—around the time that you start writing the book. This can help you avoid lost time on the back end. A good developmental editor can review your table of contents, outline, or general flow and help you develop your ideas early on so you don't have to go back and write additional pieces after the first round of edits. (We'll talk more about how to hire an editor in Chapter 12.)

USE DEADLINES TO GUIDE YOUR PROGRESS

Writers desperately need deadlines or the writing doesn't get done. And there isn't one writer I know who operates differently. With that in mind, I want you to set reasonable deadlines that motivate you and keep you moving, even in the face of resistance.

For the sake of kindness towards yourself, I'm requesting that you avoid arbitrary, absurdly short deadlines. A crushing deadline that doesn't take into consideration everything we just discovered about your schedule and your writing habits and abilities is futile at best and demoralizing at worst. However, you still need deadlines, and you need to use them wisely.

Deadlines need to be realistic. We've already discussed the way in which you arrive at a deadline, but keep this in mind as the project progresses, and you learn more about your process.

Deadlines need to have value to you. Most of my clients are initially spurred to write a book because they are speaking at a major industry event in the next year, and they want to have a book ready to sell to the audience. This is a very good motivator if the author has started the process early enough to use it (rather than three weeks before the event).

I've worked with clients who have set deadlines with other personal meanings—like they want to see their parent hold their book before they pass away from a terminal illness, or they want to have it published by their birthday. Whatever it is, it needs to give you the boost you need to keep going when doubt and resistance creep in.

Deadlines need to include accountability. I've learned the hard way that I'm not as accountable to myself as I would like to be, and my deadlines are far more likely to be met when there is someone else on the other side waiting to see my work. After many years of working with authors, I think that's true for most of us.

For a deadline to have any teeth, you need to set up a situation in which there is some kind of consequence if you don't deliver on the date you set. Whether that accountability comes in the form of an editor, a teacher, a business partner, a mentor, or an accountability buddy, it doesn't matter—it only needs to be important to you.

Deadlines can be used throughout the process. Most people think of deadlines as part of the end game. Their editor or publisher expects their draft by a certain date. But deadlines can and should be used throughout the process. Set a deadline for when you want to be done creating the first draft of your outline. Set another one for getting one section of your book done.

Accept that things will get messy. If this is your first time writing a book, accept that you're new at this and that it will be messier and harder than you think. You will make mistakes. Accept that it's okay to be new at something. Approach it with a beginner's mindset, and acknowledge that you don't have all of the answers because you've never done this before. When you've operated at a high level for a long time, it's hard to feel the insecurity of being a first-timer who doesn't know how the publishing process works. Just know that it's okay, and no one expects you to know everything.

Be ruthlessly protective of your time. As your end-date approaches, you will have to get very realistic about your energetic resources. Could you go to that party the week of your deadline? You could, yes. But how much energy will that cost you? Could you keep your standing hair appointment the day before your deadline? You could, yes. But again, how much will that cost you in energy and in time? Don't be afraid to turn down appointments, meetings, or commitments you've made. You can always reschedule and pick up the pieces when you're finished.

Plan for interruptions. Without fail, every time I've had a major deadline, something has come up: my kid or partner gets sick, a major appliance breaks down, or we have some other family emergency. This is almost guaranteed, so this means I go easy on myself and take it one step at a time. It's very easy to shift into overdrive/panic mode and go too hard, but this rarely helps. What helps is letting the unimportant stuff go, like those loads of laundry or the dishes. It helps to be okay with ordering out more than usual or with canceling plans so you can have more breathing room to rest and write.

Know when to ask for an extension to your deadline. "I love deadlines. I like the whooshing sound they make as they fly by," said writer Douglas Adams. You said you'd get it done by a certain date, and you want to uphold your word. You also just want the damn thing done. But there are times when the book truly needs more time and work before it will be ready to publish. While book professionals don't love extending deadlines, they know that it's a part of the game. In fact, most of them schedule in extra time when they plan out their publishing schedule, knowing that their authors will likely need at least one extension.

If you really feel the book is not ready, and you need more time, ask your editor what they can do to move the deadline. Just know that changing the deadline will probably change production times, and that means the publish date that you've already set (and maybe already announced) might change too.

Trust yourself to get the work done. I once took on an insane deadline for a ghostwriting project: write an entire book on a topic I know little about in three months. As you can imagine, the pressure was on. It was a deadline that could make anyone crazy, but when I felt nervous, I repeated the mantra: "The book is already done, the words are already written." In the end, that was true—right on time.

Plan significant amounts of time off after your deadline. Whether this is your first time publishing or not, the closer you get to your deadline, the harder you will work. You will be squeezing out every last idea so that your book will be the best it can be. Even the writers who have done this multiple times know that sometimes the best ideas and work come out when the greatest pressure is applied.

Assume that you will be completely drained when you meet your deadline, and plan for substantial time off so you can recover. This means that you need to plan ahead and avoid any other major project deadlines within two weeks, starting any new endeavors or projects, or planning a trip to a relative's house whom you can't stand (trust me on that one—your tolerance for contentious political conversation around the dinner table will be at an all-time low if you're burned out).

Reward yourself lavishly when you finish. Along with time off, plan to treat yourself to all of your favorite things. Personally, I love to schedule a half-day at the spa with a massage and facial. I tend to experience deadlines in a very physical way, so having a massage gets me back to a balanced state a lot faster. Another writer I know orders a very nice bottle of whiskey to celebrate his completion. Another writer shops and buys a piece of jewelry that represents what she went through to complete the book.

Maybe you love a certain restaurant or have been putting off a trip to your favorite place in the world. Maybe you just want a few days of completely undisturbed time so you can binge on your favorite Netflix show. Whatever it is, plan to treat yourself after you reach your deadline.

chapter nine

Navigate the Creative Journey: How Not to Lose Your Mind While Writing

When you start the journey of writing your book, you're starting a creative process that will take you—and eventually your reader—on a journey. It's time to take all of this rich material you've gathered over the years and translate it into words that flow, inspire, and move your readers in the same way the subject has moved you.

You no doubt know that the act of writing is a challenge. How do you take something as hard to define as a thought or a feeling and describe it on the page in a way that delivers your truest meaning to your reader?

How do you overcome your doubt, day-by-day, and continue to write? Once you've done the hard work of translating your thoughts into words, how do you organize them into a book that makes sense? Bridging the inevitable gap between what we intend to say and what we actually write is what makes writing—or any creative endeavor—challenging (and so rewarding).

Every writer goes through their own transformative, creative journey, although we may be so focused on the end-game of writing a book that we don't even think about it in those terms. Because nonfiction writing has taken on such a business-oriented air, new authors often forget that writing is a creative act. Which means that it gets messy. The work of writing a book doesn't go in a straight, clean line from point A to point Z. You will get sidetracked, distracted, and discouraged just as often as you feel inspired, excited, and elated.

Writing a book will call on everything you have. If you consider yourself to be the least creative person on earth and favor analytical thinking, you will have to call in your creative genius or your readers will be bored to death. If you consider yourself a deeply creative and artistic being, you will have to call on your analytical side to organize your creative mess, or no one will understand your message. I believe that your whole being needs to be engaged to write an effective book that moves your readers. While it isn't easy, it is achievable.

Writing a book is as much a head game as it is a matter of sitting your butt in your chair and regularly writing. You have to know how to navigate yourself through resistance, frustration, and doubt.

If you take nothing else away from this section, please remember that you will find yourself emotional about your book on some days, exhilarated on others, and, at times, downright frustrated and sick of it. You'll have peaks of triumph throughout the experience, and you'll have troughs so low that you'll think about quitting and walking away from the work altogether, even if you're near the finish line. This is totally natural, but it's the awareness of the journey that will keep you going when the going gets rough. As much as it can be frustrating, it can also be heart-warming, liberating, and exciting to write and put your work and ideas out there. By the end of your writing process, you will understand your ideas and your work so much better than you did when you started that you will be a changed person.

Now, for the practical side of things. In this chapter, I will share some pieces of advice that have helped me and the writers I coach navigate the journey. Above all, knowing how you react under pressure, how you work best, and how to nurture your creativity is going to be an incredible asset to you. If you don't yet know how you work in a creative process, then give yourself the time to learn.

SWOOPERS VS. BASHERS

One of my favorite descriptions of writers comes from Kurt Vonnegut, who once said there are two types of writers: swoopers and bashers. According to Vonnegut:

> Swoopers write a story quickly, higgledy-piggledy, crinkum-crankum, any which way. Then they go over it again painstakingly, fixing everything that is just plain awful or doesn't work. Bashers go one sentence at a time, getting it exactly right before they go on to the next one. When they're done they're done.[6]

Swoopers are those who have the big idea and have to get it all down on paper in a rush of blood and sweat and tears. They don't stop until they have everything they want to say down on paper. Then they go back and refine. The bashers meticulously labor over every sentence and paragraph until they feel it is as perfect as it can be. They enjoy choosing the perfect word to describe what they want to say, and they don't move on until they're sure they've said exactly what they want to say. Needless to say, a basher's refinement process might be a bit easier in the end, but it takes longer to get that initial draft on paper.

If you think about it, you can see swoopers and bashers in all areas of life. Most of the entrepreneurs I know are swoopers. They're the idea people, the creators with the big vision, but they're not always the ones to get it all organized and expressed in vivid detail and precise language.

Most of the bashers I know are detail-oriented and analytical to a fault. They're language-lovers and have a deep knowledge of words and what they mean. The wrong word drives them crazy, so they will labor over a sentence for what would seem like insane amounts of time to a swooper.

In my years of writing and coaching, I think Vonnegut is right —and that it's best not to work against your nature.

If you're a swooper, sit down and write your entire piece and get it all out, as messy as it might be. Hold a place for facts by using brackets like this: [NEED TO INSERT STATS ON CRYPTOCURRENCY AND CATS]. Make sure to highlight any sections that need work or refinement. Do what you can to minimize interruptions to your flow.

If you're a basher, enjoy your process. Take your time over your words and phrases, but don't get stuck if you feel it isn't perfect—perfection is a daunting standard that will never be met. If you get stuck on a word or a phrase, read it out loud to yourself. Hearing the spoken words can give you the necessary clarity to move forward or make changes where needed.

Understanding where you fall on the spectrum is not for the purpose of changing that about yourself. It's so you stop fighting against the way that you naturally create. As I mentioned in Chapter 7 when we talked about the different ways of outlining, forcing yourself into being intuitive when you are analytical or vice versa typically doesn't work. Honor the way you naturally create. If anything, think about how you might get closer to that sweet spot right in the middle, the place that combines the best traits of swoopers and bashers.

TURNING OFF THE INNER CRITIC

When you sit down to write freely, your inner critic is going to do everything it can to get you to stop writing. It will shut you down fast and hard the moment you make a mistake. If you're going to get anywhere with your writing, your critic needs to take a back seat.

Writing defies the inner critic, the voice who won't shut up long enough to let you get a thought out. The voice of your inner critic could belong to anyone: your mother, father, brother, the first-grade teacher who told you that you weren't quick enough and didn't know how to spell. Worst of all, it could be your own voice telling you that you suck at this.

There are a couple of ways to handle the inner critic, and you'll have to try out a few to see which works for you. Try the following:

Notice who it is. Do you know the voice? Is it related to an embarrassing event in your life, perhaps one that made you feel as if you were "less than" or incapable of achieving something? I'll give you an example. When I was in the fifth grade, I totally flubbed an easy word at a spelling bee simply because I was nervous and too cocky to write down the word. I was mortally embarrassed.

Afterward, another boy in my class teased me because of it, and it's his voice I hear when I doubt that I'm good enough to be a writer. It was a one-time mistake, and yet I can still feel the echoes of the mortal shame I felt when I think about it—and that was decades ago. But there's power in knowing the source of the feeling. When you can identify the voice and the story that goes along with it, you've identified (one of) the root source(s) of the problem.

Rewrite the story. You are an adult now (presumably). If you saw someone teasing another person for a mistake they made, you would stick up for them and come to their defense. Do that for yourself. Imagine telling that person what you would say. Be incredibly kind to that version of you who was hurt by the events within that story.

Put it aside and do it anyway. You know the story. You know the feelings that go with it. Now, it's time to set it aside for the moment. When it's time to write, there is no time for insecurity.

So, when you've given yourself ample time to acknowledge the feelings, it's time to set them aside and do the work anyway, no matter how you feel. Sometimes the best way to work with stuck emotions is to take action anyway, even if it feels uncomfortable at first.

You'll soon notice the discomfort fade after you show up for yourself consistently.

"Just twenty minutes." When I'm feeling nervous, stuck, or otherwise uncomfortable about writing, I tell myself that I'll write for "just twenty minutes." After that, I have full permission to stop if I'm still feeling stuck or stalled out.

I have never once stopped after twenty minutes. I'm in the flow, so I keep on going. By giving myself permission to duck out of writing only after I've written for twenty minutes, I essentially trick myself into writing.

Let it all in. Fellow writer Ramona Ausubel once told me that in the beginning, it is your job as a writer to be open and welcoming to whatever comes through your door. Whatever the idea, the phrase, the example, the metaphor, the weird story, just write it down. As author Mike Ganino says "Don't backspace yourself." It is not your job to judge it when it shows up; it's only your job to write it down and revise or edit later.

Turn your screen backlight down. Some writers get distracted by their own writing. They either notice the errors they made or feel like they should go back and re-read what they wrote, just to see if it makes sense. This sounds productive, but reading is not writing. If you find yourself distracted, try turning the backlight down so you avoid interrupting the flow of writing and killing your train of thought.

CONQUER THE BLANK PAGE

There is a rare subset of writers who find nothing more inspiring than a blank page. The freshness, the crispness. It's rife with opportunity. It's like a fresh blanket of snow. But for most of us, the blank page—with that endlessly blinking cursor—mocks our inability to find the words to start.

If you find yourself in the latter camp, don't start with a blank page at all.

In *The Artist's Way*, Julia Cameron tells us to spend the first 30 minutes of each day writing your "morning pages." The way Cameron uses them, Morning Pages are three handwritten pages of whatever drivel you've got running through your mind. It could be anything: "I'm tired and cranky, and I haven't had my coffee yet this morning," or "I'm so pissed at that rat bastard for what he did," or whatever it is that you need to get off your chest.

While I wholeheartedly endorse the exercise of sitting down to write out what you feel by hand, I've adapted this practice for my pre-writing jitters. I just type out all of the gunk that I have going on in my head. I might start out with my frustration about how cranky everyone was this morning, or my to-do list. I might write a few of the ideas that are bouncing around in my head.

Most importantly, at some point, I transition to writing about the resistance I feel toward what I need to write that day. Or I might write about how I'm not sure what to say at this particular section of the article, chapter, or book. It's a moment to get out exactly what you feel, even if you're RAGING IN ALL CAPS, but don't get caught up in having to write three full pages before you sit down to create something of value.

The number of pages is not important. It's more like cleaning out a fireplace. If you take the time to clean out the gunk, the fire can breathe.

Conveniently, writing a few lines also destroys the intimidating and pristine blank page. I find that if I sit down and start writing about whatever resistance I have to writing, I'll drift into that territory naturally. What starts out as emotional stuff turns into ideas I have about how to approach it, or ideas I want to include, or the problems I see that need to be addressed. Those moments of writing about the resistance create the opening that helps me move through it.

START WHERE YOU WANT TO START

Yet another hang-up for would-be writers: they don't know where to start when they write. Or rather, where they think they should start is the most challenging place to begin.

Here's what you need to remember: We are linear readers, but we do not have to be linear writers. Your rough draft is likely going to be rearranged in the editing phase, so don't stall yourself because you can't get your opening introduction story right.

In fact, although it's the first thing in your outline, you don't need to start with the introduction at all. I give you explicit permission to start anywhere but there. Writing your introduction should be the last thing you write because your introduction serves as the preview to the reader, and you'll know your book so much better after you've written the rest of it.

Dive in where you need to dive in. If one of your main points or chapters is easier to write about than the others because you have more content, or you're more excited about it, start there. You might start with your supporting ideas, or start by writing down your examples and going from there. Maybe you start with a particular story that you love telling or inspires you. The point is, don't let the order in which you think you should be writing stop you from actually writing.

GET UNSTUCK
Everyone experiences creative blocks. Everyone from writer F. Scott Fitzgerald to singer Adele to composer Rachmanoninoff to Peanuts creator Charles Schultz has experienced some kind of creative drought—it's not just you. It's helpful to think about what kind of creative block you're experiencing and what you should (or in some cases, shouldn't) do about it.

Recently, a friend reached out to share some of her struggles around writing. She was sure she had writer's block. She said:

> I was really enjoying writing in my blog, but lately I feel like I have nothing to say. It's definitely some sort of block. I know I'm still finding my voice, and I am trusting that this is all part of the experience, but I haven't felt inspired by anything lately. I picked up the guitar that I've been learning to play for a week and I've committed to enjoying that... I learned to play a week ago and have been enjoying it. I know I have a lot to say, a lot of life experiences I want to share, but when I try to write about it I just go blank.

There's a key element to consider here: my friend has been through an amazing and life-changing transformation in the last few years, one which involved the brave choice of leaving a comfortable life for a very different and uncertain path. In other words, she's been through a lot, and she's still going through a lot. In light of that, she first has to consider whether her lack of creativity might be less about removing a creative block and more about respecting her creative cycle.

Once in a while, life just happens. You've got a lot going on. If you're going through the birth of a child, if you've lost a loved one, if you're getting a divorce or going through a hard break-up, if you're moving—those factors need to be taken into consideration. Most of us have a tendency to say, "Well, it's not that big of a deal that my dog of fifteen years just died. I should be able to work through it," when in fact, it is a big deal.

Instead of letting it be an emotional event and giving ourselves a break, we decide that we should be able to "power through it" and write or produce anyway.

Please don't do this to yourself. If you're going through something major in life (and you are the one who gets to decide what counts as major, not society at large), give yourself time to work through it.

That being said, writing can help you process all of the emotions you might be experiencing. I'm not suggesting you force yourself to write the business book you want to publish, but I do believe that cathartic free-writing, where you allow whatever needs to come out to do so via pen and paper, can be healing. Personally, writing down what's happening inside is one of the best ways for me to make sense of what I'm going through.

Our culture doesn't make it easy to honor the creative cycle. We stress productivity no matter what, we prize the next achievement, and we want the never-ending pursuit of the goal. Life simply isn't designed this way. We have cycles of planting, growth, tending, harvesting, and death. There are times in our lives where going after a major goal feels unnatural simply because of where we are in our own cycle.

Because of our collective inability to acknowledge natural cycles, we believe we should be overflowing with something to share all the time. We think that because we wrote well before, we should always be writing well. And my friend does need to write—she's started her own business and wants to spread her message. She could be experiencing a block in the form of the pressure to perform. However, she's still internally sifting through her experience and may not be able to verbalize it yet.

The seed for what will be very inspirational material has been planted, but now she needs to wait patiently while it germinates. And that takes time. It can take months before you're ready to share the nugget of wisdom from your experiences—and that is truly okay.

Problems with The Text

Sometimes, creative blocks come from the work itself. You're stuck on one area of your text, you've revised it over and over again, and the more work you do, the worse it is.

I was ghostwriting a book and had to work on a chapter about my author's experience of mom guilt, as well as a general commentary on mom guilt in our culture. No matter what I did, I could not get this chapter right. The more I changed, rearranged, added, and deleted, the worse it seemed to be. At the time that I was writing this, I was a wee bit stressed out. It was a Saturday night, the deadline for the revision was Monday, and I was no closer to figuring it out. I had to be away from my kid all weekend to work, which made me feel like a bad mom, and I had a fight with my partner. Things felt bleak.

That night, I shared everything I was going through with a friend of mine, who is also a writer. He looked at me and said, "So you mean to say that you had an argument with the father of your child, you had to spend all day working, which meant that you couldn't be with your kid the way you think you should be… and you don't know why you can't write the chapter on mom guilt?"

With that one question, it all clicked. The chapter wasn't coming together because, on a personal level, I was struggling to grapple with the very topic I was supposed to be writing about. What's more, I was writing about it from a detached standpoint instead of embodying what I was saying. It was as if I was standing outside a room looking in, trying to describe it the way I saw it instead of owning that I should be in the room with all the other moms who feel guilty.

I had to get real with myself about my own feelings of mom guilt, what it meant to me, how it showed up in my life, and the moments that sparked it. And when I did, it became one of the strongest chapters in the book.

I've seen this pattern repeat with dozens of clients. If you're struggling with an aspect of what you're writing, get real with yourself. Sit in it. What about that topic aren't you facing? Is there something that you haven't resolved, and, yet, you're trying to teach it? Is it very present in your life somewhere, and how is it showing up? Are you failing to practice what you preach? Sit down and write about all of the ways you might actually be stuck inside of the very problem you're trying to describe, and you probably won't be stuck for long.

Sometimes we arrive at a point in the work where we realize we actually don't have enough to say. This can show up as avoidance or confusion. Some of us have a hard time admitting when we've reached a topic in our own book that we don't know as well because it feels like an embarrassing blindspot that we don't want to admit to having. This is completely normal—of course you'll know some aspects of your work better than others. The key here is not to delay in getting that information. Depending on what it is, it could take some time before you develop the material, so allowing procrastination to rule the day in this scenario only makes things worse.

As soon as you realize you need to do more research, test a theory, or gather stories or examples, get busy doing it when you're not writing. That way, this momentary snag won't become a major roadblock.

Problems will come and go. Let them. You will experience problems in your manuscript. You will know that there are deep issues with a chapter or a section or an idea. And you might spend hours or days hacking away, rearranging, or rewriting without making it better. When that happens, step back from that section and give it a rest. Move on to the next chapter or section, and focus your efforts there.

Sometimes it takes space to gain clarity. Sometimes it takes a shift in one chapter of the book to realize what you need to do to solve the problem. Realize that creative blocks often come when you are too close to the problem, meaning you are dealing with the very issue you're trying to describe on the page. And if all else fails, get a second opinion from someone in the demographic of readers you're trying to reach.

Lack of Inspiration

This is probably the most terrifying of all of the blocks. You have the time to write. You have your goals. You might even have a book deal and a publisher waiting for your manuscript. You sit down to write and… nothing. No creative spark to speak of.

First, what have you fed yourself lately? I don't mean food—I mean, what does your inspirational diet look like? Have you been reading books or articles that challenge you and cause you to think differently, or have you been binge-watching *Workin' Moms* episodes on Netflix? Have you had any stimulating conversations lately with new people from different walks of life, or have you been hanging out with the same people who tend to do the same things, day in and day out? Have you traveled, tried something new, taken on any new challenges? Are you interested and excited about your topic, or have you done it to death?

Inspiration comes in many forms, but when we talk about using inspiration as fuel for our creative work, we need to remember that there are some things that fuel us and some that deplete us. Yes, *Workin' Moms* is hilarious and makes for a good break, but I think few of us can argue that TV is supportive of our creative work. Lifelong friends are important, but it's also vital to expose ourselves to new ideas and new people. When we stretch our boundaries, we give ourselves the opportunity to make new connections and come up with creative ideas.

If you're not consciously feeding yourself a steady stream of inspiration, whatever that means to you, you'll notice an uptick in creativity when you give your creative spirit something to work with. Let's say for a moment that you are generally feeding your creative spark, but you are unexcited about writing the book. This might be a moment for brutal honesty. You need to ask yourself...

Do you *really* want to write this book?

When I meet an author who has been struggling to write a book for years and making little to no progress, this is the first question I ask. I always pay close attention to the way they answer it. Most of the time, they spend a lot of energy convincing me that they do indeed want to write this book, but their face and body language tell a different story. They really don't want to write the book. They have no enthusiasm about it whatsoever.

If I do a little more digging, it turns out that they've spent so much time and money on this project, and they've been talking about it for years, so they feel like they have to finish it. It becomes a tug of war between the belief that they should have integrity and do what they said they would do (write a book) and their deep desire (and preference) to pursue other creative projects.

If you find yourself in this camp, do yourself a favor. You have my full permission to quit. Don't stay in it because you said you would. There are tons of other creative projects and outlets that you can pursue. Don't spend another minute on something that doesn't light you up.

Burnout

Burnout is closely related to a lack of inspiration, and they can go hand in hand. There was a point in my professional career where, for three months straight, I was pushing myself hard. I was writing two proposals and finishing the final edits on a manuscript, and the pressure was heavy. By the time I finished what felt like a dead sprint, I was exhausted. I had set myself up to have a low workload for the following few weeks after the final deadline, which was fortunate because I had nothing left to give. I was suddenly left with all of this time to myself, during which I had planned to work on my own writing, but I was totally drained. And while the desire was there, I had absolutely no creative inspiration at all.

I had to be very gentle with myself, set low expectations, eat well, and above all, rest—a lot. Over the span of a few weeks of taking care of myself, my sense of excitement and inspiration returned, and I had plenty of ideas to work with.

If you've been pushing yourself hard with little rest and no time for yourself, it's going to be difficult to perform the way you want to. Take a look at the previous months, or even years. Have you given yourself time? Have you taken a break at any point? Are you getting enough rest? If the answer is no, consider how to carve out downtime so you can have the energy to foster the creative spark when it returns.

Fear

Fear often shows up as "productive" procrastination. We suddenly feel we have to do the pile of dishes, or clean the house, or pay all those bills, or even re-read and edit our previous work—anything instead of writing. This might arise if you feel an incredible amount of pressure around what you're writing. For example, you might have a book deal that you're super excited about, but now you're terrified about the reality that you really need to show up. That kind of fear, especially if we don't want to admit that we're afraid, can be crippling. There is no getting around fear until you admit to yourself what you are truly feeling.

You don't need to roll around in it or obsess over it, but you do need to acknowledge it. I hope you have some coping techniques for fear—some of us do yoga, some of us exercise, some of us meditate. I do all three when I experience fear, just to move the emotion out of my body.

How we manage fear is key. However, having a solid structure helps me act in spite of the emotion. When I have a well-planned structure, I'm able to focus on what I know needs to be written. Maybe I choose the easiest part to write, the part I know by heart, because it will be easier to accomplish. With one accomplishment under my belt, I can move on to the next section, and fear has less of a hold on me.

Having a solid structure is like a shortcut. You can tell yourself you'll just work on that one easy part for twenty minutes. By the end of twenty minutes, you're far less likely to stop.

When things get hard, or you find yourself creatively stuck or blocked, know that it's often hardest just before you're about to have a major creative breakthrough. Getting stuck in your process isn't necessarily a sign that you should give up—it's a sign that you're probably much closer than you think. Once you've taken the time to realistically align your mind and your heart with reasonable expectations, you're ready to write again.

Having a creative block doesn't mean that you're a bad writer or artist, that you're dried up, or that you have nothing left to say. It's usually only an indicator pointing at some area of your life that has been left unattended and needs attention. Make the space for yourself to acknowledge and work through your block, and you'll be creating again in no time.

EMBRACE THE SHITTY ROUGH DRAFT

Of all of the tips I've gathered over the years, this one from author Anne Lamott is the most essential: **give yourself permission to screw up.**

I really want you to mean it when you tell yourself this is the first draft, and it's going to be BAD. Shitty. Rotten. Name it the "Shitty Rough Draft," or something that acknowledges this is not going to be the best and final copy. It's like giving yourself permission to suck on the first go-round.

Lamott has authored many books, including the writing classic *Bird By Bird*, and she has this to say about first drafts:

> … Now, practically even better news than that of short assignments is the idea of shitty first drafts. All good writers write them. This is how they end up with good second drafts and terrific third drafts. People tend to look at successful writers who are getting their books published and maybe even doing

well financially and think that they sit down at their desks every morning feeling like a million dollars, feeling great about who they are and how much talent they have and what a great story they have to tell; that they take in a few deep breaths, push back their sleeves, roll their necks a few times to get all the cricks out, and dive in, typing fully formed passages as fast as a court reporter. But this is just the fantasy of the uninitiated. I know some very great writers, writers you love who write beautifully and have made a great deal of money, and not one of them sits down routinely feeling wildly enthusiastic and confident. Not one of them writes elegant first drafts...[7]

Think about this as an experiment that requires a single sentence that includes some of your ideas. Only later do you need to turn it into something shareable and publishable. The pressure to perform is so high otherwise that it's impossible to think clearly. Invite yourself to just write down some ideas and start from there.

The most intimidating part about writing a rough draft is not necessarily what anyone else will say about it, but what you will tell yourself about it.

I have a harsh inner critic, too, and I know that it's capable of ripping me apart over bad writing if I let it. When I embrace the idea that the first draft is going to suck, going to be really bad, juuust terrible, I let go of all of the expectations that I have of myself. The more often I embrace the shitty rough draft and sit my butt in my chair and write, the easier it gets.

A FINAL WORD

We've reached the point where you stop reading and start writing. It's time to put some of what you've learned to practice. While you can go to Part 4, you'd be jumping the gun a bit.

As Dr. Suess says in *Oh, the Places You'll Go*:

> You have brains in your head.
> You have feet in your shoes.
> You can steer yourself
> any direction you choose.
> You're on your own. And you know what you know.
> And YOU are the guy who'll decide where to go.[8]

It's up to you to write now. You've got what you need, and it's time to go. Good luck.

PART 4
REFINING THE FORM

Hopefully, you're only beginning this section because you've already done some writing. Maybe you haven't quite finished the book, but you're ready to think about how to approach revising your work. This is the most important part of the process because it is this process that takes a mass of words and turns it into a book. Like Michelangelo once said about carving a marble masterpiece: you are removing what is *not* the work of art.

Every writer has to go through the process of revising and improving their work. But let's make a distinction between revising and editing. You, the author, revise. You do not edit—let's leave that work to an editor.

Here's why: while you can, and definitely should, get pretty far with your own revisions, you also need to accept that someone else is going to have to help you get it to the finish line (we'll talk about editing later).

In this section, we're going to talk about how to revise your work, and then how to work with an editor to get your book ready to publish. This section will take you up to the draft that you're ready to hand over to an editor—we won't be covering interior or exterior design of the book, printing and distribution, or marketing (although there are plenty of resources available at sarastibitz.com).

There are some basic practices that will help you appraise and improve your writing before passing it off to someone else. The process can help you understand yourself as a writer at the same time that you're improving your book.

When you work with an editor, there are three parts of editing you need to understand: the structural or developmental edit, the line or copy edit, and proofreading—in that order. You'll generally take the same approach when you work through your revisions.

In the developmental review, you'll get a feel for how your ideas hang together—or don't. As an author tackling this yourself, this is often the most difficult task because it's hard to see the holes in your work when you think it is complete.

In the line review, you'll focus on the nitty-gritty details. This is where you work on word choice, sentence construction, grammar, syntax, typos, spelling errors, etc. This is also the least favorite part of revising for most writers.

After you've taken the book revisions as far as you can, you'll look for editors and beta readers to help you cross the finish line.

chapter ten

Developmental Review

The developmental review is where you truly find the gold in your writing. You may feel like you've given it your all in the writing process, and you have. But when you do the work of looking at your book from a 30,000-foot view, you'll be able to see those areas that need improvement and fix them, making your reader's journey through your book so much easier and smoother. This is where we do the heavy lifting.

Although it might seem easier to jump in and fix the small stuff like errors and typos, you'll want to make your structural edits first; this review might reveal areas where you need to cut or add content, and you don't want to do the work of line editing on content you won't keep in the end.

TIME IS ON YOUR SIDE—LET IT MARINATE

First things first: Don't jump straight into revising your book after you've finished the rough draft.

In his book *On Writing*, Stephen King describes how he waits six weeks after finishing a manuscript before editing the prose. He puts it away in a desk, locks the drawer, and doesn't revisit it again until six weeks have passed. Why? Because the book needs time to marinate, he says, and because he finds rereading his book after six weeks "exhilarating" and necessary for making the best revisions.

King's approach works because it allows him to look at his work with fresh eyes. This is crucial because fatigue is a real thing in writing. When you've looked at your work dozens of times it can become so unclear that you end up doing more damage than you otherwise would if you had given it space and time.

"But Sara," you might be thinking, "I can't possibly wait six weeks just to give it the first read-through." Remember what I said in the beginning about arbitrary deadlines? I hope you've stayed away from those.

Yes, there are those occasions where it is important to have a book ready before a big event or a breakthrough moment. But if the book simply isn't ready, it won't do you any good anyway, even if you publish it in time for that big event.

Give the book the time it needs. We don't always have six weeks to stash away that manuscript, but it bears saying that time away from your work is to your benefit. The more time you can give yourself, the clearer your perspective will be. If you don't have time to spare, there are a few things you can do to make a quick transition to revising easier on yourself.

First, take as much time away from your book as you can reasonably allow, even if it's only one week. This means hands-off, no reading, no tinkering, no fixing.

Second, when you come back to the book, consider taking it out of the context in which you wrote it. Print it out and read it on a hard copy, or if you're used to reading your document on a desktop, send the PDF to your iPad, or even change the font size and the color. This might sound silly, but it's all about making it look "fresh" to you and changing the context so you can see things in a different light.

THE READ-THROUGH

When you're finally ready to pick the book up and review it, remember that this stage can take some time. It isn't as simple as one read-through, a few tweaks, and voilà, you're done. You'll need to put the time into this process to make your work the best it can be. Most first-time authors completely underestimate the time it will take for them to make revisions to their initial draft, so plan for a couple of weeks (at the very least) to make your revisions.

As you read, keep in mind that you'll probably have to do some major rearranging of your book to make it readable and easily understandable for your audience. As I said before, we are linear readers, but we are not typically linear writers. It's unlikely you will write a book where all the pieces are in the right order on the first go-round.

When we write, we tend to jump around with our thoughts. We might have one paragraph with three thoughts on the same topic and a closing sentence that belongs elsewhere. Most of the authors I've worked with start with an initial opening paragraph that they are sure works well. However, when we edit, we find something perfectly succinct and even more to the point later in the writing. That will become the introductory paragraph.

Start by reading over the book from beginning to end. Keep the following in mind before you start:

- Don't focus so much on typos right now, especially if you have a lot of them; we'll go over those in the next section.
- Don't skip parts because you "know what they say." Trust me, you don't… When we write, we tend to stop, start, and skip around.

We might think we've explained something when we actually skimmed over it. If I'm telling myself that I know what it says, it's because I'm avoiding that section because I don't want to deal with whatever I will find. Related to this, don't skip parts because you're cringing at the thought of having to fix them. I'm guilty of this one, too, but more often than not, I'm surprised to find that the section needs only a few small changes.

- Try to keep yourself impartial about your work; don't get sucked into the emotional experience. What do I mean by emotional experience? This can mean two things: You're either so thrilled with your writing you fail to see the areas that need improvement, or you're so critical of your writing that everything looks terrible. Especially in the latter case, it can make revising feel emotionally exhausting. Remember that you gave yourself permission to write a Shitty Rough Draft, and behold, you have done so.

As you do your read-through, mark or comment on any areas to address. If you're working on-screen, use the comments function. If you're working on paper, jot down a note in the margin. Be sure to write down your initial impression of what's wrong with the section and how you'd like to fix it. You may not know the answer right away.

If I don't know how to fix it immediately, or even if I can't quite verbalize why I don't like it, I still make a note about my general impressions and remind myself to revisit this section later. Sometimes, the answer will come as I'm revising other sections of the manuscript.

Whether you've printed out the book or you prefer to read it on the screen, it's critical that you look at it from the reader's point of view. Use comments or a pen to note parts that don't work. Look for the following:

- Gaps in information or places that need more detail or explanation.
- Areas where an example or story would help to illustrate your point or bring the section to life.
- Areas that don't flow with the previous or subsequent text, where your ideas jump around, or where you repeat something you've already said.
- Statements that are vague and assume knowledge on the part of the reader.
- Areas with too much information or unnecessary detail.
- Missing transitions from section to section or chapter to chapter.
- Gaps in chronology where you skip around from one story to another out of sequence.

Ask yourself the following questions:

- Is there any content that needs to be cut? Look for distracting tangents or areas that are too thick or too advanced for the reader.
- Does it flow well, and do the parts of the book line up in a way that feels intuitive to the reader?
- Are there parts that could be moved around to make it flow more smoothly?
- Does the reader have the information they need to understand each concept at the right time?
- Is your tone consistent throughout the piece? For example, do you start out sounding like a professor and end up sounding like a comedian? And if so, does that work?
- As you are reading, are you engaged throughout the entire book, or are there areas where you feel bored or lost?
- Are there holes where you incorrectly assume your reader knows what you're talking about?

- Is there too much information in one area and not enough in another?
- Do you use research, case studies, or examples to support your ideas? Are there enough case studies or examples so that your reader understands your point? Or are there too many? Do they explicitly underscore the point you're trying to make?

Feel free to mark it up. Scribble all over it if you need to. Don't overthink it. If it feels off, circle it—even if you can't yet articulate why—and move on. Also, circle or comment on sections that you love. It's important to notice the good stuff, too. Taking a moment to appreciate your writing will be a boon to your mood should you begin feeling bad about all of the corrections.

GET TO WORK: MAKE YOUR REVISIONS

After you've finished your initial read-through, go back and make your revisions. You'll do them in the following order.

Delete. Whether you're a swooper or a basher, you likely have content that clearly needs to be cut. This one might be tough for two reasons: You might feel like you don't have enough content to begin with, or you might feel attached to words, even if they don't seem to fit the overall premise of the book.

In the first case, if you worry that the book will be short on content, that's okay. While there are areas that need trimming, you probably have areas that need to be filled out with more material. It tends to balance out in the end.

As we've discussed, you should give some thought to your preconceived ideas about how long the book "should be." Don't waste time and energy trying to hit a magic page number. It should be only as long as it needs to be for the reader to get the message. Some of the best writers I know are succinct and prize word economy over anything else. These are people who have subscriber lists in the millions. They get their message across beautifully and simply without any unnecessary words. It doesn't have to be long. It just has to be good.

In the second case, if you've fallen in love with something you've written, there's a saying in the fiction world that fits here, too: "Kill your darlings." We all have those turns of phrase, stories, or huge chunks of knowledge that seemed to flow so well in the moment or felt really important. If the phrase, section, paragraph, sentence, or word doesn't serve your reader, or if it takes you off course from the premise of your book, then it needs to go.

But that doesn't mean you have to get rid of the section of text entirely. It could serve as an article or a free downloadable that you use to attract readers to your website... or even the seed for your next book.

Move pieces around. If, during your read-through, you circled areas that needed to be rearranged, do this part next. As you rearrange, make notes or comments about the need for new material to fill in gaps that have been created or to write transitions to stitch the pieces together. You don't need to do that right now, but it helps to make a note so you keep track of future work.

If you find this part difficult, taking the work analog might help. Write down the titles of the sections in question on post-it notes, get down on the floor, and move them around relative to one another like puzzle pieces. Gauge what needs to come first, second, and third in order for the reader to grasp what you're saying.

These two steps alone often result in a book that is leaps and bounds closer to done than when you started.

Fill in gaps. Now go back and work on the areas that need improvement or more content. Start with areas where you need to fill in holes and gaps in your writing. Are there areas where you assume the reader understands a concept or idea? It's better to assume that you need to explain it. After all, they don't know what you know. Go back and fill in the information your reader needs to grasp your message. This is also a good time to go back and fill in any facts or parts where you put an [X] because you needed more information (lookin' at you, swoopers).

Next, if you identified areas where your point could use an example, select your best story, and plug it in. Be sure to keep it succinct. When I write examples, I often find I include information that isn't necessary to the reader or that I find interesting but another person might not. Use only what you need to drive the point home and skip the backstory.

Finally, are there entire sections missing that need to be written that weren't in the first draft? If so, write these next, and don't skip parts that you'll "come back to later." This is where you need to apply willpower and get the job done. As Anne Lamott says, "Butt in chair." Don't let up.

At this point, you will have done a lot of work. Take a break. You'll need a little bit of space from your book before you begin your second read-through. Again, you need time between making your revisions and rereading. How much time you need is dependent on your deadlines and what it takes for you to come back to the work with a fresh perspective.

On this read-through, make sure you have filled in all the gaps in content, rearranged the pieces that needed to be moved, and included strong examples. Make sure you have addressed all the notes you made on your first read-through.

At this point, you might be ready to dive in and make line-by-line changes. Before you move on, take a moment to celebrate before you go back at it—you've come a long way, and you deserve to take pride in your accomplishments.

chapter eleven

Line Review

After you've (hopefully) taken a break from the developmental work on the book, it's time to get into the details and fix the word choice, sentence structure, grammar, and anything else that needs to be addressed.

This is the most tedious part of editing, I'll admit. Although printing out your work is helpful for structural editing and proofreading, I strongly recommend you do your line edits on-screen.

For one thing, there are plenty of apps that can help you with this task, and for another, you'll be creating twice the amount of work if you first write your edits into your printed version and then transfer them to your digital version.

When you begin this review, ask yourself the following:

- Do your words match your meaning?
- How will your word choice land with your reader? Are there words that might distract (for example, swear words might click with some readers and distract others)?

- Do you use passive voice when you could use active voice?
- Is it too wordy? Do you say "starting to feel" or "beginning to run" when you should say "felt" or "ran"?
- Have you overdone it with adjectives and adverbs?
- What reading level did you write for? Did you write for grades 14-15, when your readers find it easier to read at grade 9?
- What stylistic habits do you notice about the way you write? Are there words or phrases you use again and again that feel redundant to the reader?
- Are there typos and misspellings that will distract the reader?

I'm not going to lay out the grammar rules—there are plenty of resources available, including *The Elements of Style* by Strunk and White and *The Chicago Manual*, in print and online (and I encourage you to use them).

What I am going to do is give you a few rules of thumb to keep in mind. I'll also share some of my favorite tools for editing, as well as the downsides of using them.

Your voice and style are important. When I edit for authors who have a distinctive voice and want to keep it that way, I make a point not to redline the hell out of their words. Sometimes a one-word sentence is appropriate to make the case. Sometimes a phrase that breaks the rules carries more meaning than one that is technically correct.

What makes a piece grammatically correct and what makes it readable and enjoyable are sometimes very different things. Some of the most well-known writers write very simply, with minimal punctuation. Some writers claim all commas are speed bumps. While I happen to like a well-placed comma, it is important to consider whether your word or punctuation choice slows or enhances the reading experience.

Take it easy on your style. You want your voice to shine through your work. Think about how to get your copy as clean as it can be without losing your personality.

Stick to active language. Never use the passive voice where you can use the active. Look for phrases that are more specific and vivid. Cut those phrases that create distance between the reader and the moment. You want them to imagine the scene as if they are there.

Here's an example of a passive sentence: "The book was written by a bestselling author." This sentence is passive because the subject (the book) is receiving the action rather than performing it, and the verb phrase "was written" uses "was" as a helping verb, signaling the passive construction.

Here's an example of an active sentence: A bestselling author wrote the book. This sentence is active because the subject (a bestselling author) is performing the action (wrote), making the sentence more direct and engaging.

Look for the simplest way to say it. It's very easy to get into what I call author-speak. You know, that tone someone takes when they feel like they have to "sound" authoritative, whatever that means to them. Aside from the fact that it generally doesn't fit their voice and isn't an authentic expression of themselves, it usually leads a first-time author to be overly wordy. You might use a five-syllable word where a one-syllable word would do. It's okay if your writing is simple—don't over-complicate the text in an attempt to sound like an intellectual.

Your reader doesn't care about your intellectualism. They only care about the transformation they will experience from reading your book.

Select the most natural word choice, but stay away from vague and overused or cliched words. A cliché is a term that is so commonly used that it has no meaning anymore and lacks vitality. Even if it's a popular term right now, take it out. You're writing a book with a lasting effect. Excluding clichés strengthens your writing and avoids premature aging of your work. Go with your instinct about the word that conveys your meaning best, and if you're in doubt, use an online dictionary and thesaurus.

Vary your sentence length and rhythm. Watch for variation in your sentence length. If you're prone to short sentences, add some variety with longer ones. If you're prone to long sentences that run on, cut them up into several sentences. Watch for the rhythm of your words.

Repetitive rhythm is wonderful when used consciously, but if you're not paying attention, you might succumb to writing in the same rhythm repeatedly. This can bore your readers, even if they love your material.

If it is possible to cut a word out, always cut it out. When we talk, and when we write, we use a lot of filler words. This is fine for stream of consciousness writing. However, when it's time to edit, these filler words should be the first to go. To start, look for too many uses of "that," "just," "really," "very," "so," and "to."

Look for repetition. You might have noticed that I start a sentence with the word "So..." quite a lot in this book. Or maybe you haven't because I've cut the majority of them out (I can assure you, there were many in the first draft). This is a word I tend to use when I'm speaking and writing to help me connect one idea to another. It's perfectly fine to have it there while I'm writing because it contributes to my state of flow, but the reader doesn't need to see it.

As you read, look for phrases, sentence structures, or words that you use far too often that have no value to the reader. Cut almost every single one of them, unless it's crucial to your style or absolutely necessary for your reader to get your meaning.

Watch for tense. When we write, we often switch back and forth between past, future, and present tense. Make sure you're staying consistent within each story, example, or explanation.

Use your senses. In nonfiction writing, particularly business or how-to, it's easy to get lost in telling people what to do. This usually means that you're missing out on the chance to engage their senses and speak to them in a way that makes them feel what you are saying. Writing is naturally ephemeral. You're trying to use words to describe an event, a feeling, an idea, or a real person, and sometimes words fall short of the goal.

Use sensory words to create a vivid picture in your reader's mind so they fully grasp your meaning. When readers can use their senses to imagine what you're describing, they retain what you say far better because the imagery you shared has much more depth.

If you want to move people, you need to help them connect to what you are saying on a physical and emotional level. For example, if I wanted you to understand my experience of trying seafood for the first time as a young child, I could write the following:

> One of my earliest memories is of sitting around a table with my parents. We are living in Spain, and my father has come home with a bag of berberechos, these tiny little clams that are no bigger than the size of a dime. You can get them by the pound at the market down by the ocean for very cheap, and he has cooked the clams in butter, wine, and garlic. Now, my mother and I join him at the table to eat clams and fresh-baked bread.

Not bad. But now let's consider this:

> My parents and I live in Spain, and my father has come home with a bag of berberechos, these tiny little clams that are no

bigger than the size of a dime. You can get them by the pound at the market down by the wharf for very cheap, and when he opens the bag to show me, I can smell the brine of the sea clinging to the shells. The afternoon heat lingers in the living room as he cooks them over the hot stove. Soon I can hear the hiss and pop of garlic cooking, the clatter of shells as they hit the pan. I sit at the table where my mother has set out ruby red tomatoes and fresh-baked bread. Our fingers are slippery as we pry apart the buttery, half-opened shells and slurp down the salty-sweet gold inside.

You'll notice that I called in sensorial experiences: smell, feel, sight, sound, and taste. I also write in present tense instead of past tense. Does the scene feel different to you?

While the first paragraph isn't bad, it's only when I read the second paragraph that I can tap into the visceral experience of this moment with my family.

The best way to practice sensorial writing is to write as you normally would. Then when you revise your work, find areas where you can add detail and sensory experience to the text. Make sure you avoid overloading the paragraph, however.

Nothing should be added that will drag down the rest of your prose—add it only if it creates a picture for your reader and helps move the story along.

Don't obsess. If you've changed the words in a sentence or a paragraph more than three times, and they're still not clicking into place, zoom out and ask yourself if these particular words are even necessary. If you feel they are needed, then reconsider where you are in the book and what it is you need to say. At some point, you need to move on and trust that your editor and proofreaders will give you feedback that will move you forward.

Follow the rules, but only until it's time to throw them out.
George Orwell is one of the seminal writers of the 20th century. You probably remember him as the author of *Animal Farm* and *1984*. In his set of essays entitled *Politics and the English Language*, his penultimate rule is: "Break any rules sooner than say anything barbarous."[9] By barbarous, he means barbaric. It's important to know the rules, but it's equally important to know when to throw them out.

Orwell's main point is this: clean up your writing. Don't slow your reader down with a speed bump created out of thick, hard-to-understand language.

TOOLS FOR GRAMMATICAL EDITING

I'm going to assume you're not a grammar snob and that you might need some help in this area. If this is not your strong suit, grammar might not be the place to spend tons of time and effort—*your* time and effort, anyway.

There are some great tools that can help you further assess your writing, which I've listed below. While these tools are not substitutes for doing your work, they can help you understand the problems with your writing faster.

ProWritingAid: This is an app I use with Google Docs, but you can download and use it with Microsoft Word, too. It's a licensed product for which you pay a yearly fee, and it's worth the price. This tool has a ton of bells and whistles, so many that it may be overwhelming to the average writer. On the other hand, you'll get an in-depth, instant take on your writing. You can choose to have the application check your grammar, style, voice, overused words, and consistency. It also checks for clichés, corporate speak, "sticky" sentences, and plagiarism, as well as many other options. You can choose to have a summary report to get a quick 30,000-foot view of your work. This software can be found online or in Google docs. For the latter, go to Add-ons > ProWritingAid > and select your report preference.

Hemingway: The Hemingway App is another great tool for checking your work, and it's free. With Hemingway, you can see the "readability" of your book—the level of education one needs to read it. You can find out easily with Hemingway whether you're writing at the 6th-grade or 12th-grade level. The app displays spelling errors, gives suggestions for cutting adverbs and adjectives, highlights passive voice, and tells you when your sentences are "hard to read" or "very hard to read." This is my favorite app for getting a quick handle on the readability of my work.

The software is very simple. There aren't a lot of bells and whistles, and the color-coding of the issues in your work makes them readily identifiable. For example, when you edit a "very hard to read" sentence and make it shorter, you'll get instant feedback when the color downgrades to yellow or disappears. This feels good. However, like Grammarly, it can be clunky if you're working on a large file. This is best for doing a tone check on a small sample of your work to get a sense of the overall readability of it.

Grammarly: Grammarly allows you to check your document for typos, grammatical errors, plagiarism, and much more. They offer free and subscription access to their app. This software also has a browser application that allows you to have Grammarly check your work as you work within your browser, no matter what application you use.

Grammarly allows you to quickly assess where you stand with your work. If your work has a lot of errors, you can turn off the rules and metrics you don't need to see to focus on one metric at a time. For example, if both the Syntax and Spelling error checks are on and you have a lot of problem areas, it might become overwhelming. Turn on one at a time so you can focus on that problem area.

Grammarly has its drawbacks; it can be clunky when you have a very large piece to edit, such as a manuscript. There's no way to sync your changes with something like Google Drive or Microsoft Word, so if you're using one of those to create your document, you're going to have to cut and paste it or download the revised document from Grammarly. This might cause you to lose any previous formatting. A better option if you're set on using this software: either use the app's browser plugin, or start your work in Grammarly and transfer over as you go. It has a function for you to save your work, and when you're finished, you can export the document to the word processor of your choice.

A word of warning: none of these software apps are error proof. Don't assume that using them will eliminate all errors, typos, or syntax issues. I regularly find mistakes the software failed to pick up—sometimes a repeated word, sometimes a phrase the software didn't understand. These apps will do a lot of the heavy lifting, but the final polish will have to come when someone proofreads the work later, at the end of the editing process.

After you've done this work, you will have reached the stage where the magic of collaboration will make your book far better than it is already.

chapter twelve

Editing and Feedback

You've finished your book, and you've done as much as you can on your own. What's next?

Now you're ready for feedback. That feedback will (hopefully) come in two forms: from an editor, and/or from a group of qualified beta readers.

There's no specific right order to getting feedback. Some authors prefer to have beta readers read the book before engaging an editor, while others prefer to have at least one round of professional editing before sharing their work with anyone. Still others skip working with beta readers all together. How you do this depends on what you need, your timeline, and your audience. In this chapter, we'll walk through what you need to know about getting the right feedback for your book. We'll talk first about working with editors.

WHY EVERYONE NEEDS AN EDITOR

Very few people truly understand what a good editor does until they've worked with one. They enter into this world thinking that they need to hire someone to give their book a "once-over." They don't realize that a good editor makes the difference between a book that sings and a book that falls flat; they can make the difference between a mess of ideas on the page and a united theme with supporting points that illustrate your experience, methodology, and overall brilliance. A good editor can find the holes in your thesis, make sure your book flows in a way that reaches your unique audience, and call out the best in you.

It's not all typos, grammar, and syntax. Remember the levels of editing I described earlier? That's what editors do—they make sure your book is developmentally and structurally sound, they make sure every line sings and says what you want it to say, and they clean up any errors you might have missed. While you've done a lot of the heavy lifting, your editor is a collaborator who tends your ideas and acts as a neutral set of eyes that will help you see things in a fresh way and catch the mistakes that you couldn't see yourself.

Everyone—from novices to professional writers—needs an editor. Why? First and foremost, you are likely too emotionally attached to see the book (and its problems) clearly. This is true for every single writer I've worked with. I meet authors who think their work is amazing and nearly complete, and authors who think their work is terrible and that I'm going to tell them they should never write again. Both camps are letting their confidence or insecurity run the show, and they are both wrong. You need an editor to help you see the book clearly and to make it the best book that it can be.

Second, by the time you're ready for editing, you will have been working on this book for a long time. You know your book better than anyone else, that's true, but this leads to a familiarity that creates blindspots.

I am no different. Even after years of editing other people's books, I couldn't see this book that you're reading clearly. It's like standing inside of the wine bottle, trying to read the label—it simply doesn't work. Just like you, I had to have other people give me feedback so that someone else can point out the holes or inconsistencies that I can't see.

Familiarity can also breed laziness. We get tired of reading the same thing again and again. We've all reached that spot in the manuscript that we don't want to revisit ... and so we skip it. Obviously, this does not lead to improved text.

The question isn't "Do I need an editor?" but "What kind of editor do I need?" Because new authors in particular come into this with the misconception that they're hiring someone to correct their word choice, most don't realize that they will very much benefit from a developmental review. You can usually find an editor who does both, or who works in partnership with someone who complements his or her skills. In many cases, hiring a proofreader is a good idea, too.

When to Hire an Editor

As discussed in Chapter 8, it's best to get your editor on board before you finish writing the draft so you save yourself the lag time. Many authors assume the editing process can be wrapped up quickly, so they believe the editing process will take a couple of weeks to complete. *Don't make this assumption.* Every editor has their own process, and if they're good and take pride in their work, they won't bend to an ill-informed deadline. If you find an editor willing to work on a short timeline, you will pay exorbitantly higher amounts than you would if you gave the book ample time for review. Worse yet, the work may not be to the standard that you want it to be.

As a general rule, you should plan to give the editing process anywhere from eight weeks to three months, depending on the length of the book and the work needed. When we work with clients, we plan for three months, which includes three rounds of review and ample time for the author to make the needed revisions.

How to Look for an Editor

If you have friends who have published a book before, start there. Ask them about their process, how they published the book, and which book professionals they worked with. You'll hear about what they liked, didn't like, and what they would never do again. Hopefully, they can give you the name of a fabulous editor.

If this fails, check out some of your favorite or most well-known books, especially those published independently. Very often, the author thanks their editor in their acknowledgments. If you like the book, you probably like the editing. Research those editors to see if they would be a good fit for your book.

Look for the following in an editor:

- What kind of experience do they have?
- How many years have they been editing?
- How do they present themselves?
- If they share content, is their writing clear and easy to understand? Is it versatile? Do you like their style of writing?
- What books have they edited?
- Does their work fall into one genre or many? Is their previous work in line with your book? If you're writing a nonfiction book, you won't want to work with an editor who primarily or exclusively works in fiction.
- What are the content, style, and tone of the books they've edited?
- How do they work with authors? What is their process, and how long do they typically take to work through each round?

Lastly, try to find out what other interests they have that might make them uniquely qualified to edit your book. For example, I practice yoga. An author writing a book on yoga, meditative practices, or things of a spiritual nature might have a better experience with me as their editor because I have a unique angle and can add more thoughtful insight. I've also been in entrepreneurial circles for a long time, so I have a unique insight into what it takes to run a business. On the other hand, my contribution to a technical manual on, say, electrical engineering, would be less insightful, as that topic is far outside my wheelhouse.

The price of hiring an editor varies widely. Some editors prefer a per-page rate, while others charge by the hour or project. In general, you can expect the following ranges:

Low: $1000 to $5000
Mid: $5000 to $15,000
High: $15,000+

Most editors will expect a percentage of payment before they start working with you, so be prepared to make an upfront investment. Only you can determine the budget that works for you, but remember that you get what you pay for.

Gauging the Working Relationship
Your relationship with your editor is important. It's so much more intimate than you might expect. Your editor is going to have a direct line into your thoughts, experience, methodology—and emotions. Editing can be stressful and emotional, just like writing. An editor will be your creative partner for this part of your book-writing journey. If they don't treat you or the manuscript with respect, the work will be harder on you.

It's okay to go with your gut. If you're hiring your own editor or in a position to choose your editor at a publishing house, listen to your intuition. It's okay to go with the editor who is newer or less experienced because she understands the nuance of your topic and shows enthusiasm as opposed to the editor with the rockstar resumé who seems condescending. Choose someone who has an understanding of the process and the emotional journey of creating a book, and who can help you navigate both.

It's important to mentally and emotionally prepare yourself to work with an editor. There will be moments where your editor tells you something you may not like to hear. As my colleague Matthew Turner says, "They *will* tear your baby apart, and it *will* hurt." You are likely to react strongly to the guidance they give. If you didn't get to choose your editor (because you're working with a publisher that assigned you one), you might find it especially hard because there might be less trust built in. If you have a good working relationship, your editor should be able to deliver the news to you in such a way that you understand their reasoning and can consider their ideas—and consider them you should. Your editor can provide valuable insight into your content.

A good friend of mine was working with an editor at a traditional publishing house and asked me what to do when he got his first round of feedback. "I feel like she's nitpicking my words. I'm ready to go to war, guns blazing. Am I off base?" he asked.

This is a completely normal feeling to have when you first see the red lines in your book. It feels like your poor manuscript is bleeding. It took you a long time to write this thing, and the last thing you want to see is someone ripping your words apart, right?

Well, in my friend's case, the editor was tightening his prose and building a case in the opening pages that would compel the reader to keep going. She wasn't really nitpicking the important words; she was cutting words like "and," "but," and "really." He couldn't quite see that from his perspective, which was one of emotional attachment. He needed to learn that working with an editor is a dance of give and take, and he needed to put away the blazing guns.

As a professional writer, my work has been edited countless times and I can attest to the embarrassing fact that my first read-through of an editor's comments is still frustrating to me. What gets easier, however, is knowing how to handle my own reactions and knowing how to gauge when to push back. I set time aside to first read-through the comments without reacting, commenting, or making any changes. Then I let the comments sink in over the next day or two while wrestling with whatever thoughts and emotions arise. Then I come back to it with fresh eyes and determine how to respond. By that time I know how I want to move forward and what questions I need answered for clarity. And, more often than not, the time and space away helped me see that the editor wasn't coming at my poor baby with a butcher's knife; she was trying to help cut away everything that wasn't necessary for the book.

However, if you find yourself in a position where you feel doubt about your editor's ability to truly help your book, it's important to say something. When an editor doesn't understand the material (and doesn't seem to be picking it up by reading your book) or doesn't understand the audience, the book can suffer. When an editor shows disrespect to the author, their work, or their ideas, that's a giant red flag. Ultimately, this is your book. You have to fight for what it needs, and if it needs a new editor, speak up.

What to Do While Your Book is Edited
You're probably thinking that now that the book is off your desk, you can go on vacay. *Of course* you can take a well-deserved vacation, but you definitely can't leave your editor hanging. You will need to be involved.

Given that your book will ideally go through two rounds of edits (or more, depending on what it needs), you will need to be responsive to your editor. When my team edits a book, we do a developmental read-through and make general notes and suggestions. We'll prepare an editorial memo for the author and meet with them to discuss it, so they're clear on what they need to do next—i.e., write more content, clarify an idea, fix the voice, add research, etc. We'll also agree on the flow of the book.

At this point, the book is back in the hands of the author, who will spend the next few weeks rearranging content, adding additional material, and doing the work we requested. Generally, the author has the book for anywhere from two to six weeks to address the requested changes and suggestions.

When the author passes the book back to us, we start the line edit, assuming the developmental stage is complete. We won't do this until we have all of the additional content needed from the author. We continue through the revisions by passing it back and forth between the author and our team. See why it's important to stay engaged?

While you're waiting for your editor to get back to you, you can work on your title, cover design, and marketing copy for the front and back covers. You can start to flesh out your marketing plan and get some of the moving pieces in place. You can build your book's webpage, or pull together resources that you'll share along with the book. You can also spend time gathering testimonials and blurbs from current and former clients or supporters to help promote the book. This is not an idle time; use this time and space to prepare yourself for the launch ahead. Go to sarastibitz.com for resources.

WORKING WITH BETA READERS

After you've completed one or all rounds of editing, you can begin to share the book with a carefully selected group of readers. This is the point in the process where, ideally, you're bursting with excitement about your book, and you're super eager to send it to everyone you know. You might even be thinking about sending it to your mom, your dad, your brother, and your best friend.

Please don't.

For so many reasons, this is a bad idea. First, it's highly unlikely that your family and your best friend are members of your target audience. Second, if they have a judgmental, critical, or insecure bone in their bodies, they may tear your book apart for reasons that have nothing to do with the strength of your work. That's the last thing you need. You need feedback, but it's absolutely critical that it is constructive feedback, and you may not get it from that corner of your life.

The reason authors share their work with beta readers is to get constructive feedback on the manuscript before it's published; this work helps the author understand whether the book does what they intended it to do. That means the people giving the feedback need to be qualified to do so. Ideally, your beta readers are:

- Professional writers and editors
- In your target audience
- Your mentors or people who have experience and knowledge of your industry, target audience, ideas, and content

Anyone outside of those three buckets might do your book (and ego) more harm than good. While there may be people outside those groups who read the book, these are the people whose opinions will be well-formed and based on objective knowledge, not personal opinion.

A beta reader is a person who fits your ideal audience demographic and, usually, has a deep understanding and interest in your work. If you already have a following, this could be someone who has been watching your work for a while. If you have clients and a customer base, maybe this is a client who has been your loudest supporter. The basic idea of this process is to get high-level feedback rather than line-edit-level comments, but some beta readers do take it on themselves to point out errors and typos.

Your group of beta readers could include just three to five people, or it could be up to 50 (or more), depending on your access to a pool of potential readers. Keep in mind that the more early readers you have, the more work you'll do to review and collate edits and suggestions. You also run the risk of having "too many cooks in the kitchen," meaning that you get conflicting advice that is difficult to implement. The upside is that you could get valuable feedback about the knowledge you share and the way you've organized.

Think about the people in your life who would make helpful beta readers. If you have ten in mind, expect five to seven to say "yes." Of that group, only two or three are likely to give you feedback. When this happens, try not to take it personally. It has nothing to do with the book or your relationship with that person. Usually, it's because your beta readers have good intentions but are, like everyone else, overcommitted.

There are a couple of aspects you need to think through before you ask your beta readers for feedback:

1. **How much time will you give them?** You want to give them enough time so they feel a slight amount of pressure, but not so little time that they feel resentful or can't get it done. This could mean two weeks for a shorter book, or four weeks for a lengthy or technical book. Give them a very clear deadline.

2. **What kind of feedback do you want?** Beta readers are best for high-level feedback. As such, ask them to comment on the areas they loved, liked, hated, or felt bored by. Also ask them to point

out areas that felt unclear or confusing. You can get granular and ask them if a particular story or chapter works, but know that when you ask them to focus on one area, it may come at the cost of them reading the rest of the book.

3. **How will you collect the feedback?** For a small group of beta readers, consider giving them a comment-only copy of your latest draft on Google Drive and let them comment where they have questions or remarks. If you go this route, you'll have to consider whether you want them to be able to see each other's comments or not. You could also use a Google survey. Periodically follow up with them throughout the time that they're reading the book. Most people need a gentle reminder here and there. Also keep in mind that this is a great way to gather early reviews for your book; just remember to ask them if it's okay to use their comments in promotional materials. And finally, be sure to thank them for their effort—they've just given you precious time to help you make the book better.

Proofreaders

Proofreaders are those final readers who read through your manuscript to ensure the bits and pieces have been cleaned up and are ready for print. Ideally, a good proofreader is someone in the writing profession or someone in your ideal audience with a detail-oriented eye for typos.

This final read-through should happen after your work with your editor is finished. Your editor will likely work under the premise that the work will be truly polished and completed when they are done, and that's wonderful, but even the best editor can miss small details. Unless the editor has someone on their team who will read the text with fresh eyes, there's a good chance that reading fatigue will impact the final product. When someone reads the same text again and again, their mind can skip over extra words or look over small mistakes because they "already know" what it says. It's not something we do consciously, and editors are not excluded. That's why it's a good idea to have a proofreader go through one more time and read your book.

IT'S TIME TO CELEBRATE
And... that's it. You're done with your edits. Easy, right? Ha. I know it wasn't easy, and you deserve a big "congratulations" if you made it to this step. So many authors give up halfway through writing the book, not to mention the editing process. Congratulations—you are one step closer to becoming a published author!

I insist you go celebrate. Whatever it is that you do to celebrate your wins, whether it's spending time alone, visiting family and friends, hunkering down at home with a glass of whiskey, or buying yourself a week-long retreat, go do it. You deserve to celebrate this huge milestone.

chapter thirteen

Crossing the Finish Line: How to Know When You're Done

When is the book finally done? Many a writer has spent weeks or months laboring over the crucial points they were trying to make in the book, adding and deleting case studies, and agonizing over whether the book is "done" long after the deadline has passed. Case in point: It took me four years to finish this one, despite writing and editing many other books for clients in the meantime. What can I say? My business is based on my writing, and I'm not immune to insecurity and second-guessing, and I don't regret giving my book the extra time it needed to develop.

At some point, you have to let it go. Because the truth is, the book is never going to be done. As we've said, writing a book is a transformative process, though we tend not to think of it in those terms. That means that your emotions are going to get involved in this process, whether you like emotions or not.

If you, like so many of us (myself included), have any sort of limiting belief about whether your work is "good enough" or "worthy enough," it will be very difficult to know when it's time to let it go… and then follow through and actually let it go. If you have perfectionist tendencies… Well, that's going to be extra tough. But here's the good news: The book is never going to be done.

The really wonderful thing about book writing is that it tests your methodology and ideas on paper. Many of my clients are speakers or have been teaching their ideas for years. They've never put it down on paper *ad nauseam*, however, and they've never had to explain it in such a way that a reader who knows nothing of their topic will get it. So when they do it for the first time, they see the holes in their thinking or areas for improvement.

It's an iterative process at its best: you take an idea from one medium (the stage) to another (paper) and you see all kinds of ways that your ideas, teachings, and message can be improved. As a result, you too are changed—you are better at what you do at the end of your book process than you were at the beginning because your ideas have been tested and polished.

You, the creator, will evolve through the process of making the book, and will continue to do so. But the moment you hit publish, the book will already feel as if it's old news, or as if it's not up to your standards—because you will have evolved past it. You might not be able to get around this, but you can reframe it.

First, think of it like this: Your book is really just a snapshot of you at one moment in time. As prolific writer Seth Godin says, "A book is a physical souvenir, a concrete instantiation of your ideas in a physical object, something that gives your ideas substance and allows them to travel." It's the best you can do at the moment that you hit publish or send your final draft to your publisher. Let it be that snapshot, and accept that it will never be perfect.

Second, it's okay that you haven't included everything you know right now. Some of your readers will be ready for your newly acquired advanced knowledge, but most of them will still need the simplified version. They don't need everything—they need the most important pieces of knowledge that will get them the result they are seeking.

Third, don't let perfectionism dictate your process. When we seek perfection we lose perspective—it becomes all about us and our personal needs. If we can forget ourselves and focus on the reader who really needs our book, we can move past this and remember that someone out there is waiting, maybe even begging, for your wisdom. Instead of letting perfection stop us or keep us from releasing our work to the world, we can remember the person who needs our help and let it go.

Besides, the book will never, ever, ever be perfect. Every book on your shelf is filled with "mistakes" that the author cringes over every time she or he thinks about them, but you have never noticed. Here's writer James Baldwin on finishing a book:

> You never get the book you wanted, you settle for the book you get. I've always felt that when a book ended there was something I didn't see, and usually when I remark the discovery it's too late to do anything about it.... What happens here is that you realize if you try to redo something, you may wreck everything else. But, if a book has brought you from one place to another, so that you see something you didn't see before, you've arrived at another point. This then is one's consolation, and you know that you must now proceed elsewhere.[10]

My hope for you is that by the time you reach the end of your journey, you will have learned something about yourself, the way you like to create, and your work—and that what you have learned brings you a sense of joy and contentment.

So, when is the book done? Perhaps a better question is this: when is your book ready to meet the world? The answer lies in your willingness to let it go—imperfect as it may be—into the hands of the readers who need it. The act of releasing it is an act of bravery, one that transforms not just your story but the way you see yourself as a writer. Trust the work you've done and take the leap. The world is waiting.

conclusion

A Final Word of Advice

As I said at the beginning of this book, writing is one of the most crazy-making, frustrating, enlightening, breathtaking, exciting, and terrifying tasks one can take on. There will be moments when your writing feels transcendent and inspired and moments when you wonder how you've become a bottomless source of meaningless drivel. It's all part of the journey, and the more you can embrace the suck and the transcendence together, as two sides of the same coin, the more you will enjoy the process. Know that every writer experiences this ride, and it's your ability to move through it and continue writing that makes you a true writer.

I hope this book has provided you with some insight along your journey, and I hope that, if nothing else, you are at least inspired to put it down and write. And if you ever need help, please don't hesitate to reach out. Find more information and resources at sarastibitz.com, or email me directly at sara@sarastibitz.com.

Sara

Acknowledgments

Books are never created in isolation. This one emerged from countless conversations, collaborations, and connections that have shaped both my understanding of the writing process and my approach to guiding others through it.

To my extraordinary team: Faith Smith-Place and Steff Ho, whose organizational genius keeps our client projects running smoothly, and whose patience with their unpredictable leader is never-ending (at least it seems that way). Thanks especially to Faith for contributing deeply to this book and its development, for kicking my butt and telling me to finish the damn thing… and for walking with me during the hardest time of my life.

Thanks to Brianne Sanchez and Matthew Turner for being wonderful collaborators and colleagues through the years; thanks especially to Matthew for reading an early version of this book and providing helpful feedback.

To my clients, who trusted me with their stories and allowed me to be part of their journey from idea to published author: you've taught me more than you know. Each of you has left an indelible mark on these pages.

Special gratitude goes to Joey Coleman, whose friendship and partnership led me down a new path and taught me so much about excellence, perseverance... and what it takes to succeed in the face of incredible challenges. Thanks for being a friend.

Thanks also to Derek Coburn. Our work together changed my view of the world and my view of collaborating. It's not an overstatement to say that our partnership rescued my writing career. I'll never forget that our friendship started with an email subject line that read: "Jesus, mushrooms, and insurance."

Thanks to Raegan Moya-Jones, who inspired me with her story and her grit, tenacity, and pluck.

Thanks to Alan Yang, who has shown me what it is to be principled and generative in a world that seems to operate against those very qualities.

Thanks to Tyler Wagner, who (gently) shoved me into the world of books.

Thanks to Jim Kwik, Sloane, Dan Chuparkoff, Zvi Band, Chris Hutchins, Katrina Bos, Joe Mechlinski, Randi Braun, Eric Rozenberg, Michael Crom and Joe Hart, Paul Mills, LaShondra Mercurius, Lucian Harris-Gallahue, Meredith Fineman, Chris Schembra, Matthew Clifford and Alice Bentinck, Mike Amato, Errol Doebler, Tony Paustian, Erin Rollenhagen, Ryan Hawk, Thatcher Wine, Mary Lyn Jenkins, Adam Carroll, Mark Schacknies, and so many more. Each of you has inspired and taught me something about writing, creative work, or collaboration. Thank you.

To the members of my writing community at Zenith. Thank you for showing up every day. For encouraging me... and calling my bluff when needed. Our weekly sessions have become a sanctuary. Thanks especially to Joey Beech for being a long-time client and friend, and to Matthew Smith for being my heretic guide on a path that is no-path, and for graciously fielding all of my "Is this terrible?" texts and requests.

To the publishing professionals who've become cherished colleagues: Berit Coleman, whose talent, kindness, and patience are unparalleled. Thanks for your early feedback on this book, and for being a wonderful co-pilot when we get the opportunity to work together.

To Elizabeth Marshall, who also provided early feedback on this book and has become a friend in the trenches of the book world. Thanks for your grounded wisdom.

To Leah Trouwborst (currently at Crown), who saw potential in me and called it out.

To my first writing mentor, Catherine Knepper, who generously opened so many doors for me, endured my ranting and raving as I learned the ropes, and who still shares much-needed laughs over drinks when needed. Thank you, thank you, thank you.

To my family: Ryan and Lily, I love you Googleplex(infinity). To mi familia, Thelma, Juan, Nati, Ari and Maya, te quiero mucho. To Marci and Terry, thanks for supporting, watching Lily, listening, and encouraging me through the years. Tom, thank you for being like a second father. It means more to me than I can say. To Chelsey and Austen, Val and Craig, Amy and Tim, Jaren, Joey, Emily and Kailey, I love you all very much.

To Steve and Angel Lyle, thank you for your love, support, and guidance. My life has changed irrevocably for the better since you came into it. And Steve, thanks for the last-minute read-through. I appreciate the time and care you took to help make this a better book.

Mom & Dad, thank you for instilling in me a love of reading, learning, and traveling, even if it's only with a book in my lap. You've left me a rich legacy.

To those I may have missed: know that your fingerprints are on these pages too. Book-making is a collective endeavor, and I'm profoundly grateful for every conversation that helped bring this work to life.

Endnotes

1. "Karen Russell: A Brutally Honest Accounting of Writing, Money, and Motherhood," December 17, 2020. https://www.wealthsimple.com/en-ca/magazine/karen-russell.
2. David Moldawer, "The Audience Trap," *Maven Game*, March 7, 2020, email newsletter.
3. Pessoa, Fernando. *The Book of Disquiet: The Complete Edition.* New Directions Publishing, 2017.
4. Munger, Charles T. "A Lesson on Elementary, Worldly Wisdom as It Relates to Investment Management and Business." In *Poor Charlie's Almanack: The Wit and Wisdom of Charles T. Munger*, compiled by Peter D. Kaufman. Donning Company, 2005. Originally delivered as a speech in 1994.
5. Garrett, Keith A. "Neil Gaiman's Writing Habits." *Keith A. Garrett* (blog), January 5, 2016. http://keithgarrett.com.dream.website/2016/01/05/neil-gaimans-writing-habits/.
6. Vonnegut, Kurt. *Timequake*. New York: G. P. Putnam's Sons, 1997.
7. Lamott, Anne. *Bird by Bird: Some Instructions on Writing and Life.* Anchor Books, 1994.
8. Seuss, Dr. *Oh, the Places You'll Go!*. Random House, 1990.
9. Orwell, George. Politics and the English Language. United Kingdom: Renard Press Limited, 2021.
10. "The Art of Fiction No. 78." 1984. https://www.theparisreview.org/interviews/2994/the-art-of-fiction-no-78-james-baldwin.

Writing Tools & Resources

Writing resources and tools mentioned in the book include:

The Mission of Art by Alex Grey
On Writing by Stephen King
Thinking Fast & Slow by Daniel Kahneman
A Technique for Producing Ideas by James Webb Young
The Artist's Way by Julia Cameron
Bird by Bird by Anne Lamott
Elements of Style by Strunk & White
The Chicago Manual of Style by University of Chicago Press
Politics and the English Language by George Orwell
Creativity: Unleashing the Forces Within by Osho

Sara Stibitz is a *New York Times* and *Wall Street Journal* bestselling collaborative writer and creative coach. Many of her clients' books have won awards from Nautilus, Bloomsbury, Axiom, Reviewers Choice, Indie Excellence, and Independent Press. She has a keen ability to draw out meaningful stories from within her clients and brings a blend of empathy and intuition to every project. To learn more about her work, go to sarastibitz.com.

Don't forget to go to sarastibitz.com to get all of the downloadable templates and guides mentioned in this book, and to learn more about how you can get support in writing your book.

www.ingramcontent.com/pod-product-compliance
Lightning Source LLC
Chambersburg PA
CBHW020540030426

42337CB00013B/926